Crime & Criminals

Opposing Viewpoints

David L. Bender & Bruno Leone, Series Editors

Claudia Debner, Book Editor
Terry O'Neill, Book Editor
Bonnie Szumski, Associate Editor
Lynn Hall, Editorial Assistant
Pat Jordan, Editorial Assistant

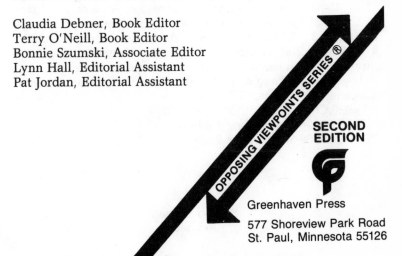

OPPOSING VIEWPOINTS SERIES ®

SECOND EDITION

Greenhaven Press

577 Shoreview Park Road
St. Paul, Minnesota 55126

Library of Congress Cataloging in Publication Data

Crime and criminals, opposing viewpoints.

(Opposing viewpoints series)
Bibliography: p.
Includes index.
1. Crime and criminals—Addresses, essays, lectures.
2. Criminal justice, Administration of—Addresses, essays, lectures. 3. Crime prevention—Addresses, essays, lectures.
4. White collar crimes—Prevention—Addresses, essays, lectures. 5. Gun control—Addresses, essays, lectures.
I. Debner, Claudia, 1951- II. Title: Crime and criminals, opposing viewpoints. III. Series.
HV6028.C68 1984   364   84-13624
ISBN 0-89908-346-3 Library Edition
ISBN 0-89908-321-8 Paper Edition

Second Edition
Revised

"Congress shall make no law . . .
abridging the freedom of speech,
or of the press."

first amendment to the U.S. Constitution

The basic foundation of our democracy is the first amendment guarantee of freedom of expression. The *Opposing Viewpoints Series* is dedicated to the concept of this basic freedom and the idea that it is more important to practice it than to enshrine it.

180973

Contents

Why Consider Opposing Viewpoints?

"It is better to debate a question without settling it than to settle a question without debating it."

Joseph Joubert (1754-1824)

The Importance of Examining Opposing Viewpoints

The purpose of the Opposing Viewpoints Series, and this book in particular, is to present balanced, and often difficult to find, opposing points of view on complex and sensitive issues.

Probably the best way to become informed is to analyze the positions of those who are regarded as experts and well studied on issues. It is important to consider every variety of opinion in an attempt to determine the truth. Opinions from the mainstream of society should be examined. But also important are opinions that are considered radical, reactionary, or minority as well as those stigmatized by some other uncomplimentary label. An important lesson of history is the eventual acceptance of many unpopular and even despised opinions. The ideas of Socrates, Jesus, and Galileo are good examples of this.

Readers will approach this book with their own opinions on the issues debated within it. However, to have a good grasp of one's own viewpoint, it is necessary to understand the arguments of those with whom one disagrees. It can be said that those who do not completely understand their adversary's point of view do not fully understand their own.

A persuasive case for considering opposing viewpoints has been presented by John Stuart Mill in his work *On Liberty*. When examining controversial issues it may be helpful to reflect on his suggestion:

> The only way in which a human being can make some approach to knowing the whole of a subject, is by hearing what can be said about it by persons of every variety of opinion, and studying all modes in which it can be looked at by every character of mind. No wise man ever acquired his wisdom in any mode but this.

Analyzing Sources of Information

The Opposing Viewpoints Series includes diverse materials taken from magazines, journals, books, and newspapers, as well as statements and position papers from a wide range of individuals, organizations and governments. This broad spectrum of sources helps to develop patterns of thinking which are open to the consideration of a variety of opinions.

Pitfalls to Avoid

A pitfall to avoid in considering opposing points of view is that of regarding one's own opinion as being common sense and the most rational stance and the point of view of others as being only opinion and naturally wrong. It may be that another's opinion is correct and one's own is in error.

Another pitfall to avoid is that of closing one's mind to the opinions of those with whom one disagrees. The best way to approach a dialogue is to make one's primary purpose that of understanding the mind and arguments of the other person and not that of enlightening him or her with one's own solutions. More can be learned by listening than speaking.

It is my hope that after reading this book the reader will have a deeper understanding of the issues debated and will appreciate the complexity of even seemingly simple issues on which good and honest people disagree. This awareness is particularly important in a democratic society such as ours where people enter into public debate to determine the common good. Those with whom one disagrees should not necessarily be regarded as enemies, but perhaps simply as people who suggest different paths to a common goal.

Developing Basic Reading and Thinking Skills

In this book carefully edited opposing viewpoints are purposely placed back to back to create a running debate; each viewpoint is preceded by a short quotation that best expresses the author's main argument. This format instantly plunges the reader into the midst of a controversial issue and greatly aids that reader in mastering the basic skill of recognizing an author's point of view.

A number of basic skills for critical thinking are practiced in the activities that appear throughout the books in the series. Some of the skills are:

Evaluating Sources of Information The ability to choose from among alternative sources the most reliable and accurate source in relation to a given subject.

Separating Fact from Opinion The ability to make the basic distinction between factual statements (those that can be demonstrated or verified empirically) and statements of opinion (those that are beliefs or attitudes that cannot be proved).

Identifying Stereotypes The ability to identify oversimplified, exaggerated descriptions (favorable or unfavorable) about people and insulting statements about racial, religious or national groups, based upon misinformation or lack of information.

Recognizing Ethnocentrism The ability to recognize attitudes or opinions that express the view that one's own race, culture, or group is inherently superior, or those attitudes that judge another culture or group in terms of one's own.

It is important to consider opposing viewpoints and equally important to be able to critically analyze those viewpoints. The activities in this book are designed to help the reader master these thinking skills. Statements are taken from the book's viewpoints and the reader is asked to analyze them. This technique aids the reader in developing skills that not only can be applied to the viewpoints in this book, but also to situations where opinionated spokespersons comment on controversial issues. Although the activities are helpful to the solitary reader, they are most useful when the reader can benefit from the interaction of group discussion.

Using this book and others in the series should help readers develop basic reading and thinking skills. These skills should improve the reader's ability to understand what they read. Readers should be better able to separate fact from opinion, substance from rhetoric and become better consumers of information in our media-centered culture.

This volume of the Opposing Viewpoints Series does not advocate a particular point of view. Quite the contrary! The very nature of the book leaves it to the reader to formulate the opinions he or she find most suitable. My purpose as publisher is to see that this is made possible by offering a wide range of viewpoints which are fairly presented.

David L. Bender
Publisher

Introduction

The causes of crime have been debated since the advent of the earliest societies. Greek philosophers such as Aristotle delved into the nature of crime and its possible causes. The debate has continued through several civilizations because *causes* are the crux of the entire social issue of crime. If a specific cause of crime could be found, then eliminating that cause would be a major step toward eliminating crime. However, if there are no specific causes of crime, then society's efforts might better be expended in identifying criminals and protecting the rest of society from them.

A recurring topic in the search for the cause of crime is poverty. It was publicly supported as long ago as 500 A.D. by a Roman statesman, Flavius Cassiodorus, who called poverty the "mother of crime." However, the Greek philosopher Aristotle was an opponent of this theory. In one of his works, *Politics*, he concluded that "the greatest crimes are caused by excess and not by necessity." In the mid-twentieth century, the popularity of poverty as a cause of crime in America culminated in President Johnson's war on poverty. A few decades later, social spending had increased dramatically, but so had the crime rate. Thus, the question remains—do social expenditures bear any relationship to the rate of crime?

Some criminologists embrace the theory that "criminals are born, not made." If criminals could be isolated by a genetic factor, say the proponents of this theory, then preventing crime would be reduced to incarceration. An attempt to distinguish criminals by appearance was made as early as the 1800s by the celebrated Italian criminologist Cesare Lombroso, who wrote that criminals could be detected by their handle-shaped ears and crooked noses. Even though Lombroso's simplistic theory was debunked, researchers are continuing to seek a link between genetic makeup and crime. A 1980 study by the University of Maryland shows a possible link between an inherited deficiency of trace metals in the blood of juvenile delinquents and their criminal behavior. Attempts to correct the chemical deficiency through chemical supplements and diet modification are showing some positive results.

Recent statistics seem to indicate that the problem of crime is reaching alarming proportions. According to the FBI Uniform Crime Reports, serious crimes showed an overall 10 percent rise in 1980. In one year, robbery increased 20 percent and burglary, 14 percent. The US Census Bureau's semi-annual survey of crime victims found that every year almost one in three US households is hit by crime. The importance of an informed opinion in understanding the questions of crime is paramount to controlling crime. *Crime and Criminals*, a major revision of the successful 1977 title, endeavors to present current issues in the timeless debate on crime. The views of prominent criminologists are juxtaposed with personal, first-hand views of prison inmates and victims to give the reader a realistic view of the arguments, both pro and con.

The first chapter, What Are the Causes of Crime? provides a foundation for the remaining chapters: How Should Criminals Be Treated? How Can Crime Be Reduced? How Should White Collar Crime Be Controlled? and Would Gun Control Reduce Crime? Each of these subjects deals with the causes of crime and criminal behavior and finally, with the elusive question of crime prevention.

What Are the
Causes of Crime?

"Poverty. . .and crime go together. That is the truth."

Poverty Is a Cause of Crime

Mark Green

Mark Green is president of the Democracy Project, a nonprofit, nonpartisan public policy institute established to critique conservative public and political policy and to develop progressive alternatives. A few of the areas of interest to the Democracy Project are economics and democracy, citizens' access to government, and crime. Mr. Green, a lawyer and journalist, is the author of *Winning Back America* and the 4th edition of *Who Runs Congress?* In the following viewpoint, Mark Green explains why he believes that economic conditions make it necessary for the poor to survive by criminal means.

As you read, consider the following questions:

1. Why does the author think that more prisons are not a feasible answer to the rising crime rate?
2. How does Mr. Green justify his claim that poverty is a major cause of crime?
3. According to the author, how is the unemployment rate related to the crime rate?

From *Winning Back America* by Mark Green. © 1982 by Mark Green. By permission of Bantam Books, Inc. All rights reserved.

The worry over crime is not the contrivance of reactionary demagogues. The burglary rate in the U.S. is 100 times that of Japan. The number of homicides in the District of Columbia is twice that of Sweden and Denmark combined. Based on the number of reported crimes in New York City in 1980 (710,153) and the presumed ratio of reported to unreported crimes (one to one), the average resident can expect to be the victim of crime once every five years. Yet the number of police has fallen by one-third in ten years, state jails are full, and 99 percent of persons committing felonies will never serve time in a prison.

To be sure, the actual incidence of crime has held steady over the past six years, according to the Justice Department's National Crime Survey. But its continuing high absolute level has created a *fear* of crime that seems to be both rising and scaring people almost to death. One 1981 survey indicates that, due to the fear of crime, 79 percent of people never carry much cash, 64 percent are afraid to go out alone at night, 50 percent think the police won't protect them, and 31 percent carry a gun or other weapon to protect themselves. Americans lose their freedom when they become hostages to their fear of assault.

Rough Justice

To deal with these "mean. . .guys with macho complexes," in the words of the director of police in Memphis, some of our conservative leaders propose to out-mean and out-macho them with a return to rough justice. Republican Senator Alfonse D'Amato, for example, suggests that we execute anyone convicted of vandalizing a church. And in July of 1981, President Reagan's Task Force on Violent Crime issued a set of recommendations for "sweeping changes" in the criminal justice system. The principal recommendations were: 1) use preventive detention; 2) modify or abolish the exclusionary rule; 3) eliminate parole for federal prisoners; 4) build more prisons; and 5) give technical assistance and training to state and local authorities. Unfortunately, the first four will do nothing to stop violent crime.

Aside from violating the principle of "innocent until proven guilty," preventive detention is the blind man's bluff of criminal justice. Judges guess wrong more often than right in predicting future crime, according to Professor Alan Dershowitz of Harvard Law School. He calculated that less than 10 percent of all crimes are committed by persons out on bail, a fraction of which are violent, and a further fraction of which are predictable. Preventive detention is probably prohibitively expensive to use, as well. President Nixon's legacy of preventive detention to the District of Columbia proved all but worthless because it requires a guarantee of "speedy trial." But a jurisdiction that has the resources—police, prosecutors, judges—to effect "speedy trials" does not need to hold the accused during a long wait for trial.

Vice-President George Bush has attacked the "exclusionary rule," which forbids police to use illegally obtained evidence at trial, because of "the ruthless killer who cleverly avails himself of the exclusionary rule." Cleverly? Exactly how does a "ruthless killer" trick police into obtaining and using illegal evidence? Of course, this rule protects all Americans from illegal searches and seizures, not just the hypothetical villains of Mr. Bush's vivid imagination. In addition, this rule—which the federal government has managed to live with since 1914—has virtually no impact on the outcome of trials. Senator Patrick Leahy (D.-Vt.), a prosecutor for eight years, says he didn't see a single crook go free because a court excluded illegally obtained evidence.

Employment Doesn't Stop Crime

"They was making $200 a day in the street, $150 a day, gambling, stealing. And now they gonna work, ten hours a day, seven days a week for $125?"

Such reasoning supports the economists' claim that, for some, crime is a rational economic activity. It appears that employment alone has only a slight, temporary effect on criminal activity among youths who are involved in property crime. Employment must be good enough (either pay enough or offer the promise of advancement) to compete with life on the street.

Michelle Sviridoff and James W. Thompson, *Crime and Delinquency*, April 1983.

Where it has an impact is before trial, as a factor in the DA's decision to prosecute or otherwise dispose of a case, usually through plea-bargaining. But in the most crime-ridden jurisdictions, prosecutors are forced either to bargain for a guilty plea or else drop the charge in the vast majority of cases—as many as 90 percent in New York—because the system cannot afford the time and cost of a trial. As with preventive detention, the answer is not to violate the Constitution, but to strengthen the practical operation of the system by adequate funding and administration.

As for longer sentences for federal prisoners, who comprise only six percent of the total prison population, violent street crime is not a federal offense. Longer sentences for *non*-federal offenses are simply not feasible given how little jail space there is now. Should we then engage in a massive effort to increase prison space? Other than the U.S.S.R. and South Africa, the U.S. already jails a greater proportion of people than any industrialized country. It costs up to $100,000 *per bed* for a maximum security prison, and up to $30,000 a year to house one felon; and it takes five to seven years to plan and build a prison. According to the National Council on Crime and Delinquency, it would cost $3 billion to build enough prisons, and $1 billion a year to staff and run them, to reduce street crime by ten percent. Brighter street lamps could probably cut crime as much, and at a small fraction of the cost.

If these approaches won't work, what will?. . . .

Breeding Ground

Poverty obviously doesn't excuse crime, but it does just as obviously breed it.

A study by Professor Harvey Brenner of Johns Hopkins University for the Joint Economic Committee indicates that a one percent increase in unemployment is associated with an increase of 4.3 percent in selected crimes (robbery, burglary, larceny, narcotics offenses, and homicide).

For example, the one area of assault which *has* been increasing at a head-spinning pace is robbery, up 20 percent in 1980. The only major property crime to track robbery's record is burglary—up 14 percent in 1980, and climbing at a consistent rate around the country. It should not take a criminologist to suggest why these two crimes should work in statistical tandem. Robbery shares with other violent crimes the presence of a victim, but it shares with burglary the singular motive of money. When people are not or cannot otherwise be absorbed by the economy, they may resort to burglary or its more primitive street cousin, robbery. It is neither slander nor alibi to suggest that in a time of economic dislocation, some of the poor will find it necessary or expedient to make ends meet in predatory ways.

Your City

Former Attorney General Ramsey Clark explained this point with some eloquence in *Crime in America:*

> Take a map of any city—your city—and mark the parts of town where health is poorest. . . .
> Find the places where life expectancy is lowest—seven years less than for the city as a whole—where the death rate is highest—25 percent above the rate for the entire city. . . .Mark the areas where illiteracy is above 15 percent, where three-fourths of the people do not finish high school, where the average period of formal education is four years less than for the city as a whole.
> Find now the parts of town where the average per capita income is 60 percent of the average for the city as a whole, where—as in the Hough area of Cleveland and Watts in Los Angeles—average individual income actually declined between 1960 and 1965, while, nationally, individual income rose 13 percent.
> Then mark on your map the areas where the oldest buildings and houses stand—those that average twice the age of all the structures in the city. . . .
> Finally, mark the highest crime areas on the map of your city.

Now look at the map of your city. You have marked the areas where there are slums, poor schools, high unemployment, widespread poverty; where sickness and mental illness are common, housing is decrepit and nearly every sight is ugly—and you have marked the areas where crime flourishes. Behold your city—you have marked the same places every time. Poverty, illness, injustice, idleness, ignorance, human misery and crime go together. That is the truth.

In his highly publicized speech on crime in 1980, Chief Justice Warren Burger complained about being "misled by cliches and slogans that if we but abolish poverty, crime will also disappear." But as Federal Judge David Bazelon emphasized in response, the link between economic conditions and crime is unarguable. In Bazelon's view, ultimately crime can be reduced only by reducing the conditions that help produce it—poverty, prejudice, and poor housing, health, and nutrition.

"Most poor people, in fact, do not steal; poverty does not compel criminality."

Poverty Is Not a Cause of Crime

Frank Morriss

Frank Morriss is president of the Colorado Catholic Academy in Denver. He has a B.S. from Regis College in Denver and a Doctor of Laws from Georgetown University. He is a contributing editor to *The Wanderer*, a national Catholic weekly publication. His books are *The Divine Epic* and *The Catholic as Citizen*. In the following viewpoint, Mr. Morriss disputes the argument that poverty breeds crime. He uses historical examples to illustrate his view that there is no connection between poverty and crime.

As you read, consider the following questions:

1. Why does the author think that existence of crime in the US is not a result of poverty? Do you agree?
2. How does Mr. Morriss use the French Revolution as an example of poverty and crime?
3. What does the author think is the risk of citing poverty as the cause of crime?

Frank Morriss, "Lack of Virtue, Not Jobs, at Root of Social Unrest," *The Wanderer*, December 16, 1982.

One of the nation's highest union leaders has suggested the acceptability of street riots in the face of unemployment. He in fact went beyond that to consider that such violence should actually be fomented. Strangely, there was little or no unfavorable comment from the media, which are always quick to report what they consider extremism on the part of those with whom they disagree. . . .

The idea seems to be that the existence of poverty and other real or imagined injustice automatically condemns the nation and its culture in which those evils exist. Added to that is the conclusion that violent means are legitimate to the change or even overthrow of that nation and its culture.

When public assertion is made of those ideas, including the suggestion of mass violence, we have at the least, dangerous demagoguery, and at the worst, incitation to criminal activity. Great Britain's democracy barely survived it in the past century when the Chartists tried to impose their theories in the streets in an exercise of mobocracy. Whatever the realities of the evils that gave such extremism an excuse, neither good moral or philosophic thought supported it. But such thought may not be available to protect us today!

A Good Society

I well know the moral principle that the right to necessities exists for a person in a state of dire or utter need. In that case the property right of goods such as food, shelter, clothing resides in the person desperately needing them. That is far from saying the poor may take the property of others, or that those unemployed may force upon a nation their idea of a desirable political system that provides jobs and economic support for all under every circumstance. One reason is that such a system is impossible. Work is response to a need, not something to be pretended or imposed. Any reasonably free system will face fluctuation of needs and therefore the risk of some temporary unemployment. It is the government's role to see to the greatest practice of justice, and it is the individual's (private sector) role to see to the practice of charity that reflects love of neighbor. Those have sufficed, if not to create a perfect society, at least to create a good society.

When such efforts are employed they leave no excuse for rioting or revolution in favor of a less free system of rigid economic control. Nor have peoples appreciative of freedom ever seriously considered such possibilities. It is no time to resort to demagoguery in their favor. To do so is to put or seek to put this country on a totally alien path of class conflict, division, and ultimate disaster. It is historically and philosophically un-American. It greatly exaggerates real problems into unsurmountable problems that must be met with a Jacobin solution where our traditions and our liberties will go to the guillotine, or fall to the mob.

Poverty Does Not Breed Criminals

Discussing the problem of crime, Prof. Ralph Slovenko pointed out that crime feeds upon the error that it is caused by poverty, or other injustices and inequities:

> "Poverty is the most frequently cited cause of crime, but crimes committed for money needed desperately to feed a family are singularly absent from our criminal docket. Most poor people, in fact, do not steal; poverty does not compel criminality. During the Great Depression, the streets, homes, parks, and subways were safe—at a time when college professors sold apples on the street and all Americans were dreadfully deprived. There was no unemployment insurance for the millions of unemployed, and no Social Security."

This may be applied to rioting and revolution as well. If the people take to the streets it will not be poverty that sends them there. It will be philosophic and political demagoguery which lures them there, just as those things put far-from-poor students into the streets in the 1960s. Poverty didn't cause the looting in Washington recently. . . .The *idea* of rioting and looting produced that violence, an idea planted and nurtured by enemies of democracy and freedom.

Affluent Youths Commit Crimes Too

Nowadays, crime blurs social boundaries, as cops in affluent suburbs learn while breaking up gangs of thieves from well-off families.

The liberal explanation used to be that poor kids broke the law because they were poor. Now the story is that rich kids break the law because they are neglected by their parents.

The truth is that most poor kids and most rich kids—neglected or not—don't break the law for the simple reason they think that is wrong. Who breaks the law are those who have convinced themselves that they are special and superior and that what they are doing is not wrong.

Nick Thimmesch, *Human Events*, February 25, 1984.

The French Revolution was not the result of poverty. It was the result of class hatred, jealousy, power seeking on the part of such demagogues as Marat, Robespierre and the rest of those radicals who wanted authority that was not theirs and rule of which they were incapable.

If all freedom of economic enterprise disappears in this country and we have the old failed experiment of full welfarism foisted upon us, it will be the work of those who distrust freedom, who trust power and hunger for it, and who are jealous of the success that freedom cannot bestow in complete equality.

There is a wide range of legitimate difference on politics, economics, society. But this range must not abandon proper liberty; the fundamental rights of justice, which includes both the opportunity of work and the right to acquire property as the fruit of such labor; respect for human nature; reward for legitimate ambition; etc. The French Revolution went far beyond those moral imperatives. There are many in our own country today who seek a new revolution for this country, and one that is not compatible with what our forefathers accomplished, but is more like the revolution of the anti-religious radicals of the French Revolution.

An Appeal to Temptation

Unfortunately, some religious spokesmen and leaders will attempt to give legitimacy to those ideas. They will insist that through control and further regulatory legislation, all poverty can be eliminated. They favor forced redistribution of wealth. They find all poverty as the result of injustice on the part of the rich, and thereby appeal to the temptation to class conflict. They have deserted the work of charity as insufficient or somehow degrading for its recipients.

Unfortunately, the American Revolution with its freedom and the amazing result of that freedom is not likely to be repeated. If Americans are ever convinced it is not worth the effort to keep it, there will unlikely be any getting it back.

That freedom is not perfect. It has not brought some egalitarian utopia. But it is still unmatched for success in behalf of the greatest number of citizens in all of history. At the worst moments of our economy, Americans are better off than others at their best moments. We could adopt the welfarism of Sweden, or the USSR, or the Chinese "People's Republic," or what Great Britain tried and has retreated from; or we could revive on some massive scale the New Dealism of the 1930s, when the depression lingered on year after year until Pearl Harbor. But we would still not have utopia, and we would have surrendered the most valuable instrument of justice available—liberty.

"A very large percentage of all lower-class
youth, including the whites, engage in some
criminal activity."

Age Influences
Criminal Behavior

Charles R. Morris

Charles R. Morris is the former secretary of social and health services for Washington state, where he administered the prison
system, and also worked for the British Home Office on police
and court administration. In the following viewpoint, Mr. Morris explains why he believes that the large proportion of
teenagers in the baby boom years caused the rapid increase of
crime in the 1970s.

As you read, consider the following questions:

1. Why does the author believe that crime compounds racial
   discord?
2. According to the author, in what age group does the incidence
   of criminal behavior peak?
3. In the author's estimation, what will happen to the crime rate
   in the next decade?

Charles R. Morris, "As U.S. Population Grows Older, the Crime Rate Drops," *St. Paul
Dispatch*, April 25, 1984. First appeared in the *Los Angeles Times*, reprinted by permission
of the author.

One of the brightest social portents of recent years has been the gradual leveling out of the crime rate. Crime statistics are notoriously imprecise, but FBI data, victimization studies and big-city police reports all point in the same direction: The rate of violent crime seems to have flattened out after about 1975 and for the last several years has actually been slowly dropping.

Grounds for judging why crime rates crest and ebb, and why the current decline in the crime rate may persist for a long time, begin to emerge from some research carried out by the Vera Institute of Justice, a small New York City foundation that has distinguished itself for 20 years by careful research into practical measures for crime control and criminal justice reform.

The devastating impact of the crime explosion of the 1960s and 1970s on American society is almost impossible to overstate. The wave of violent street crime, particularly muggings and robberies, has made large sections of most American cities virtually uninhabitable. The economic costs of crime—official and unofficial police and security forces, expensive metal grates over store windows, burnt-out hopes of abandoned buildings—pale beside the spiritual costs: empty parks and streets where people are afraid to stroll, old people barricaded behind their apartment doors.

Impedes Racial Reconciliation

Perhaps most important, since almost all violent street crime is committed by black and Hispanic youth, the crime problem has been a major bar to racial reconciliation. It provides an empirical underpinning to parents fighting school integration and allows predatory real estate "blockbusters" to destroy neighborhoods and turn a quick profit by playing upon white fears of minority crime. This ignores the fact that victims of minority youth crime are overwhelmingly minority men and women.

The Vera research, which documents a kind of street-level cost-benefit analysis of crime, concentrates upon three groups of crime-prone youth in different New York City lower-class neighborhoods—one white, one black and one Hispanic. The most striking finding is that a very large percentage of all lower-class youth, including the whites, engage in some criminal activity, usually starting with stealing and burglaries. In all three neighborhoods, the crime rate was particularly high among the younger boys, peaking at about age 16-17. And in all three neighborhoods, crime tended to be committed close to home, usually within a one-mile radius.

The major difference between the white neighborhood and the other two was that social controls were brought to bear much sooner in the crime cycle. Storekeepers or factory owners who had been burglarized often took vigilante measures against the offending youngsters or cooperated in turning them in to the police. Interestingly, the same sanctions were invoked in the minority neighborhoods, but because of the lower degree of social cohesion, it took much longer for them to take effect. By that time, the more adventurous youths had already broadened their range into muggings and street robberies.

Violent Retaliation

Almost all the offenders, however, viewed street crime as high-risk. Most of the young men interviewed worried about violent retaliation by victims and, for all the perceived ineffectiveness of the criminal-justice system, took the risk of arrest very seriously. By the time they reached 18 or 19, most of the minority youngsters were already dropping out of the crime cycle.

There was also an important, but indirect, link between crime and employment. For the younger boys in all three neighborhoods, there were more opportunities for low-level criminal involvement than there were jobs. Relatively few of the 16- and 17-year-olds worked at all.

Youths Need Conventional Ties

The Center for Action Research reports, "The only important conventional affiliations for most young persons are the school and the family. When these deteriorate, there is usually nothing left. In practice, many youth do not even have the luxury of two independent affiliations." The number of conventional ties open to young people should be increased. An obvious option is through employment.

Mark W. Cannon, *Vital Speeches of the Day*, August 15, 1981.

As the youngsters grew older, the more they worked the less they offended, but there was no clean dividing line between becoming employed and being a criminal. Most alternated between sporadic work activity and episodic criminal involvement for extended periods, with only a gradual tapering off of criminal activity. But by the time they reached their 20s, the vast majority of young men were working; only a small percentage became hardened career criminals.

It was also clear that the better jobs available in the white neighborhoods—usually through relatives and friends—was a major contributing reason for white criminal activity terminating sooner. Interestingly, in none of the three neighborhoods did public employment programs appear to play any significant role as an alternative to crime.

There are a number of implications that can be drawn from the Vera research. In the first place, police crack-downs or tougher sentencing policies, by themselves, have no more than a marginal effect in reducing crime rates. There are simply too many offenders to be incapacitated.

The implications for tougher sentencing policies are also ambiguous. On the one hand, tougher sentences may increase the perceived risk of continued offending, encouraging young men to go straight sooner. On the other hand, since few 16- and 17-year-olds end up as career criminals anyway, lengthy incarcerations, for all but the most serious offenders, are probably a waste of public resources and could well push even more young men toward hardened criminality.

The data also underlined the importance of healthy economic growth. Public employment programs are no substitute for the ready availability of a wide variety of jobs in the private employment market.

The pressure of numbers seems to create an amplification effect. There was a sharp increase in the number of young men in the last two decades. The number of black youths, in particular, more than doubled. As police and traditional social control systems proved unable to cope with the attendant increase in youthful criminality, more youngsters were encouraged to try crime, which swamped the system that much more and increased the odds again in favor of the offenders.

Recent Declines

Just as the rise in crime wasn't caused by increased police leniency, the recent declines have little to do with increased toughness. It is just one of the first glimmers of the social dividends the country will reap in the next decade from the decisive shift in its age structure already under way.

Barring massive immigration, the total number of young men in the country should drop some 20 percent between 1980 and 1990. The declines among minority youth will be somewhat smaller but still substantial.

The same amplification effect that made the crime wave of the 1970s such a horrendous plague should operate in the reverse direction in the late 1980s and the 1990s. With an older and more productive population, in fact, the 1990s could well turn out to be a peaceful, prosperous and possibly gray and conforming decade—somewhat like the 1950s. A little dullness perhaps will be a welcome change.

"Inborn chemical imbalances may underlie some of the severest criminal violence."

Heredity Influences Criminal Behavior

Janet Raloff

Janet Raloff received a B.A. and M.A. in journalism from the Medill School of Journalism, Northwestern University and is policy/technology editor for *Science News* magazine. She received the first place in magazines award from the National Association of Science Writers for her three-part feature on the effects of electromagnetic rain on nuclear fallout. In the following viewpoint, Ms. Raloff reports on research she feels links violence to abnormal levels of trace elements in criminals.

As you read, consider the following questions:

1. Why does the author think that hair research may reduce criminal violence?
2. Why is it important that criminologists separate their subjects into two general categories?
3. What does the author suggest is the link between hair analyses and criminal violence?

Janet Raloff, "Locks—A Key to Violence?" *Science News*, August 20, 1983. Reprinted with permission from SCIENCE NEWS, the weekly newsmagazine of science, copyright 1983 by Science Service, Inc.

"The first people I really got to know well at Stateville Prison," William Walsh recalls, "were people who had been on death row—some of Illinois' most famous murderers. I wondered what made people like this."

During business hours, Walsh labors as an analytical chemist at Argonne National Laboratory, just west of Chicago. But for the past 17 years, his spare time has been devoted to working with inmates of correctional institutions in Illinois. The Prisoner Assistance Program, for instance, which he founded 11 years ago, arranges for volunteers to visit inmates and to help parolees find employment; it even stages prison art shows to help creative detainees earn both money and respect.

It was as a result of these endeavors that Walsh found himself asking the inevitable: What is it that drives people to commit such reprehensible acts that they must be isolated from society, shut in behind bars? Research he's just completed—part of the growing field of bio-behavioral research—suggests inborn chemical imbalances may underlie some of the severest criminal violence. . . .

Hair Analysis

Initial attempts to sleuth out the chemistry behind violence, by examining blood and urine, proved unsuccessful. Body levels of the elements that most interested Walsh (based on his surveys of published research) were too low to register cleanly in these tests. "Then I read about the work some people had done at McGill University in Montreal, Canada, on hair analysis," he recalls.

Before long, Walsh had joined the burgeoning ranks of researchers examining hair. And his studies, reported for the first time on May 15, at a small symposium convened by the Schizophrenia Foundation of New Jersey's Brain Bio Center, indeed show a provocative link between extreme violence and the levels of certain key trace metals in hair.

"Hair has about 200 times the concentration of trace elements in it that blood does," explains Robert Thatcher, a researcher investigating the effects of trace metals on behavior at the University of Maryland—Eastern Shore, in Princess Anne. Thatcher points out that, within hours or days, almost any substance entering the bloodstream has been broken down, used, eliminated or stored within the body. So blood is only an indicator of recent exposures. To study chronic, long-term exposures, one must turn to hair.

Metabolic Disorder Link

Walsh wanted to investigate whether there might be some factor relating to inborn body chemistry—perhaps a metabolic disorder—which predisposed its victims to violence. He suspected that if such a metabolic problem led to the selective retention or malabsorption of certain elements in the diet, hints to that condition might appear as skewed elemental abundances in hair.

For his first experiment, Walsh chose 24 pairs of male siblings between the ages of 8 and 18. "I selected pairs where there was a very delinquent, violent kid in the same family, in the same house, eating the same food with an 'all American boy'—a kid who had never been in trouble, who was an excellent student, and whose incidence of violence was zero," Walsh explains.

Chemical Imbalances Cause Crime

"It is startling to break down violent people into two groups by chemical analysis. That degree of consistency is almost unknown in the study of behavioral disorders." Currently a small number of the violent subjects are being treated by Dr. Carl Pfeiffer, director of the Princeton Brain Bio Center in Princeton, N.J. "They are all doing beautifully," Walsh said. "There are major personality changes. The sociopaths, for instance, become nice people instead of being ferocious all the time."

Wilbert Rideau and/or Billy Sinclair, *The Angolite*, November-December 1983.

From each subject, half a gram of hair was shorn from an area close to the scalp. (Because hair deteriorates after growing out of the head, the interior tissue of strands several inches from the scalp cannot be trusted to reflect true hair chemistry. What's more, pollutants can invade hair; the longer the hair, the more likely it has been contaminated.) For obvious reasons, Walsh rejected anyone whose hair had been chemically treated.

Trace Metal Analyses

Hair samples were sent to one of two local laboratories that not only provided commercial trace-metal analyses using atomic-absorption mass spectroscopy, but that also permitted Walsh to calibrate their devices with the standard reference materials he had acquired. (Those included certified materials—such as tree leaves purchased from the National Bureau of Standards—for which precise elemental compositions were known.)

At the labs, hair was cleansed, rinsed with triple-distilled water, dried, weighed and dissolved completely with acid. Then a known fraction of the standard was injected into one of the spectral analyzers and obliterated at temperatures exceeding 5,000°C. Photomultiplier tubes scattered about the interior of the spectral analyzer's chamber—tuned to the characteristic wavelengths of specific elements (such as iron or phosphorus)—recorded the emissions as a sample was "zapped," to quantify its elemental abundances.

Walsh's calibration experiments showed either laboratory could be trusted to reliably measure only 11 elements. Thus he was limited to monitoring calcium, magnesium, sodium, zinc, copper and phosphorus "with high accuracy," and potassium, iron, manganese, lead and cadmium with what he terms "acceptable accuracy." Occasionally he looked at lithium and cobalt too, though he laments he hasn't been able to get good numbers on either of them in more than a year.

As analyses came back, Walsh pulled out results for standard reference materials which he had sent along. Because each sample had been coded, "there was no way anybody at the labs could tell whether one was a test sample, a standard, or a control," Walsh claims. But if Walsh found that the wrong value had been obtained for an element in the standards, he threw out all readings for that element from the tests run at a lab that day. (He would also notify the lab of the problem. Subsequent analysis might show a photomultiplier tube was mistuned or had failed.) Finally, identifications of the sibling pairs were decoded and their data compared, element by element.

Clear Results

"The results were quite clear," Walsh says. Not only did the hair from all 24 of the violent boys register abnormal readings for the elements examined, but also the levels exhibited were nonrandom, falling into one of two distinct groupings.

Relative to levels Walsh previously recorded for normal individuals, both of these violent groups were extremely high in lead, cadmium, iron and calcium; extremely low in zinc (lithium and cobalt too, whenever the data were available). But whereas one group also exhibited high levels of sodium and potassium, coupled to low levels of copper, the other group displayed "just the reverse." (Phosphorus levels, Walsh found, didn't correlate with anything.)

Most important, *none* of the nonviolent siblings exhibited either of these patterns. Since brothers ate similar if not identical diets, Walsh suspected the radical difference in elemental ratios that characterized the violent youths indeed resulted from a chemical imbalance or metabolic disorder.

Sociologists and criminologists who study violence separate their subjects into two general categories—episodic criminals and the so-called sociopaths. An episodic personality may appear absolutely normal for long periods, then erupt suddenly into extreme violence. By contrast, the sociopaths (normally referred to now as "antisocial personalities") are consistent in behavior, frequently becoming "career criminals." This personality differentiation is important because the two trace-metal patterns Walsh identified among the violent siblings distinguished between these two classes of violent behavior. . . .

Sibling Test

The sibling test "was a scouting experiment," Walsh says. "It formed the basis of a hypothesis to be tested."

That second phase of testing began in 1978. It involved 96 extremely violent men and 96 nonviolent counterparts (controls) who had been matched to the violent group by age, sex, race, socioeconomic status and whether they lived in an urban, suburban or rural setting. In each group, one-third were blacks, one-third Hispanics and one-third of European heritage. To ensure that any measured effects were not just artifacts of the prison environment (such as trace-metal content of the water supply), the violent group included not only residents of Stateville and Menard prisons, but also individuals who had left prison at least two years earlier, or who were juveniles and first offenders that had yet to see the inside of a jail.

Abnormal Makeup

Scientific excitement is focused on findings that suggest there is something different about the brains of future criminals from the start, that the physiological makeup of a killer is abnormal.

Several studies of twins and adopted children suggest there is a genetic factor, and Dr. Elliott Gershon, chief of psychogenetics at the National Institute of Mental Health in Rockville, Md., describes recent findings as "clear and provocative" evidence.

Lois Timnick, *The Los Angeles Times*, June 26, 1983.

Participants ranged in age from 8 to 62 (with a median age of 33), and individuals were considered violent for the purposes of this study only if they had deliberately and repeatedly harmed another human physically. To be classed nonviolent, one must *never* have hurt another deliberately, even as a child.

Two Patterns

Results from this more demographically diverse group confirmed what had been found earlier with the siblings. "In looking at the violent people," Walsh told *Science News*, "all but four exhibited one of the two patterns identified in the sibling study;" 35 were type A, or episodic; 57 type B, or antisocial personalities. Three controls also showed those patterns, he added, "so it was not a perfect discrimination—but it was pretty darn close."

What's intriguing, he says, is that those four violent participants whose hair exhibited neither of the original two patterns "were also peculiar and identical: They were very, very low *in absolutely every nutrient*—which usually means that they do not process food properly. And in fact," Walsh points out, "they were all very slender people."

Cobalt was initially the most powerful predictor. "We took a group of violent people and controls and found you could practically predict their degree of violence from cobalt concentrations," Walsh says—the lower the levels, the more violent the individual. However, he says, "It's been frustrating; we haven't gotten good cobalt analyses in three years." (Cobalt analyses require a special procedure and are harder to do.) Moreover, Walsh has reason to suspect the cobalt correlation may not be spurious. Cobalt is a central element in vitamin B-12. In scouring the literature, he discovered vitamin B-12 has been linked with several mental disorders.

The Maryland Team

Like Walsh, Robert Thatcher at the University of Maryland has been using hair analysis in studies to identify the effects of toxic metals on behavior. The metals Thatcher has focused on—lead and cadmium—were both abundant in hair taken from Walsh's violent subjects. In a study reported in *Archives of Environmental Health* last year, Thatcher and co-workers found a significant correlation between elevated levels of those metals and low scores on tests measuring intelligence and school achievement for 149 children on Maryland's rural Eastern Shore.

Particularly interesting was a difference in effects attributable to each metal. Lead related more strongly to reduced "performance" (knowledge- or experience-based) IQ, whereas cadmium seemed to diminish "verbal" (or innate) IQ.

In a related study, Thatcher and colleagues found hair cadmium correlated with the proportion of refined carbohydrates in the diet of 184 children studied. (Refined carbohydrates include white sugar, white flour, white rice, white pasta and synthetic "instant" potatoes.) What it amounted to, says Thatcher, was "the higher the proportion of the diet attributable to junk food, the higher the amount of cadmium in their hair." The scientists also reported that scores on tests to measure full-scale IQ, verbal IQ, performance IQ, reading and math appeared to have been adversely affected by the proportion of refined carbohydrates in the diet.

To date, the Maryland team has examined more than 500 children with a battery of tests—including computerized analysis of brain waves and "evoked potentials" (which essentially record brain-reaction time), together with assessments of school achievement, intelligence and motor coordination. Though Thatcher acknowledges he has not yet focused on heavy metals and violence, he told *Science News*, "We're going to try to discriminate violent offenders from siblings, similar to what [Walsh] did, based on a set of biological measures such as hair and brain waves."

Promising Work

The Health Research Institute (HRI), which Walsh founded in Clarendon Hills, Ill., has begun a program to send some of the extremely violent youths identified through Walsh's work to get a complete metabolic workup at major medical centers. HRI's goal is to identify the specific conditions that caused the unusual trace-metal hair patterns observed in the violent cohorts. The next step will be to see if treating these conditions in any way mitigates a boy's violent behavior. Until statistically significant numbers of subjects are tested, and until Walsh is able to control for possibly confounding variables, he won't elaborate on results of this program—except to say, "This work is *very* promising."

The Classic Criminal

What exactly is it that is transmitted from parent to child? Researchers say it may be the autonomic (involuntary) nervous system, which is thought to play a part in the early shaping of behavior.

The classic criminal's callousness, lack of remorse, inability to learn from experience or punishment, failure to anticipate the consequences of certain acts and seeming inability to "feel" is mirrored by objective physical measurements such as skin conductance tests, pulse rates, chemical levels in the blood, and brain wave tracings—all of which suggest that his nervous system is different, if not deficient.

Lois Timnick, *The Los Angeles Times,* June 26, 1983.

Walsh anticipates that one of the key questions of those reviewing his work will be whether or not his hair analyses are valid. "There are a lot of irresponsible people using hair analyses," he acknowledges, and as a result, the credibility of legitimate researchers using the technique often suffers by association.

As a procedure, hair analysis certainly has had a colorful history. The British pioneered the technique in 1922, using it to determine mineral levels in mummies. But it has found most widespread use in forensics. Since its introduction there a half century ago, hair analysis has been providing crime-scene investigators with a fingerprint-quality matching tool. Each individual's unique combination of diet, metabolism and environment ensures that elemental abundances identified in one hair sample will match only those hairs produced by the same individual.

Credibility of Hair Analysis

Outside forensics, however, the credibility of hair analysis has come into question. Criminologist Alexander Schauss, director of the American Institute for Biosocial Research in Tacoma, Wash., explains why: About 15 years ago, certain commercial labs—not the "good ones"—began allowing nonprofessionals to use their services, he says. At about the same time, he recalls, "you started seeing ads in national magazines where people could send in $25 and a sample of their hair to have it analyzed." The problem, Schauss points out, is that the ads made impossible claims—"you know, that it [hair analysis] can predict osteoporosis, or show someone's got cancer." Even with a detailed medical history, hair analysis cannot do those things.

At least as irresponsible, Schauss believes, was the fact that the ads didn't describe limitations of the test, nor explain precisely how to cut hair (even use of the wrong shears can contaminate hair). What's more, laboratory techniques and accuracy varied considerably. Notes criminologist Stephen Schoenthaler of California State College-Stanislaus, "You could take two identical samples of hair, send them to different labs and come up with two separate sets of results. It made for a holy nightmare." As a result, says Schauss, "By the late 1970s, the medical community was ready to hang anyone doing hair analyses."

But things are changing. In 1981 researchers in the field published a standardized protocol for hair analysis, spelling out exactly how to cut and analyze hair. And this year Schauss finished a four-year survey of what constitutes "normal," healthy hair.

On his own, Walsh has also been trying to advance hair analysis techniques to improve their accuracy and reliability. "And I think we have succeeded," he told *Science News*. "We [HRI] have the world's only hair standards—large numbers of hair samples for which we know precise elemental concentrations."

In fact, Walsh anticipates that within a decade or two, trace-metal analyses of hair will be as common a medical screening procedure as blood tests are today. Hair analysis provides a noninvasive and relatively inexpensive way to view physiological events.

"There are specific reasons for the nation's incapacity to keep its street crime down. Almost all of these reasons can be traced to the American criminal justice system."

America's Justice System Causes Crime

Roger Rosenblatt

Roger Rosenblatt is a senior writer for *Time* magazine. He received a Ph.D. from Harvard, where he taught English and American Literature. Mr. Rosenblatt has been honored by the American Bar Association and the Overseas Press Club for his essays. He was awarded both the George Polk Award and the Clarion Award for his 1982 *Time* cover story on "Children of War." In the following viewpoint, Mr. Rosenblatt blames the crime rate on a criminal justice system he thinks is debased by plea bargaining, low conviction rates, lack of prison space, and lenient juvenile justice.

As you read, consider the following questions:

1. What are some of the major problems that the author sees in America's legal system?
2. What does the New York Police Commissioner mean when he says, "The criminal justice system almost creates incentives for street criminals"?
3. According to the author, what is the major drawback to the juvenile justice system?

Roger Rosenblatt, "Why the Justice System Fails," *Time*, March 23, 1981. Copyright 1981 Time Inc. All rights reserved. Reprinted by permission from Time.

Anyone who claims it is impossible to get rid of the random violence of today's mean streets may be telling the truth, but is also missing the point. Street crime may be normal in the U.S., but it is not inevitable at such advanced levels, and the fact is that there are specific reasons for the nation's incapacity to keep its street crime down. Almost all these reasons can be traced to the American criminal justice system. It is not that there are no mechanisms in place to deal with American crime, merely that the existing ones are impractical, inefficient, anachronistic, uncooperative, and often lead to as much civic destruction as they are meant to curtail.

Why does the system fail? For one thing, the majority of criminals go untouched by it. The police learn about one-quarter of the thefts committed each year, and about less than half the robberies, burglaries and rapes. Either victims are afraid or ashamed to report crimes, or they may conclude gloomily that nothing will be done if they do. Murder is the crime the police do hear about, but only 73% of the nation's murders lead to arrest. The arrest rates for lesser crimes are astonishingly low—59% for aggravated assault in 1979, 48% for rape, 25% for robbery, 15% for burglary.

Even when a suspect is apprehended, the chances of his getting punished are mighty slim. In New York State each year there are some 130,000 felony arrests; approximately 8,000 people go to prison. There are 94,000 felony arrests in New York City; 5,000 to 6,000 serve time. A 1974 study of the District of Columbia came up with a similar picture. Of those arrested for armed robbery, less than one-quarter went to prison. More than 6,000 aggravated assaults were reported; 116 people were put away. A 1977 study of such cities as Detroit, Indianapolis and New Orleans produced slightly better numbers, but nothing to counteract the exasperation of New York Police Commissioner Robert McGuire: ''The criminal justice system almost creates incentives for street criminals.''

Police & Prosecutors

It is hard to pinpoint any one stage of the system that is more culpable than any other. Start with the relationship between police and prosecutors. Logic would suggest that these groups work together like the gears of a watch since, theoretically, they have the same priorities: to arrest and convict. But prosecutors have enormous caseloads, and too often they simply focus on lightening them. Or they work too fast and lose a case; or they plea-bargain and diminish justice. The police also work too fast too often, are concerned with ''clearing'' arrests, for which they get credit. They receive no credit for convictions. Their work gets sloppy—misinformation recorded, witnesses lost, no follow-up. That 1974 study of the District of Columbia indicated that fully one-third of the police making arrests failed to process a single conviction. A study released this week of 2,418 police in seven cities showed that 15% were credited with half the convictions; 31% had no convictions whatever.

The criminal justice system is also debased by plea bargaining. At present nine out of ten convictions occur because of a guilty plea arrived at through a deal between the state and defendant, in which the defendant forgoes his right to trial. Of course, plea bargaining keeps the courts less crowded and doubtless sends to jail, albeit for a shorter stretch, some felons who might have got off if judged by their peers. And many feel that a bargain results in a truer level of justice, since prosecutors tend to hike up the charge in the first place in anticipation of the defendant's copping a plea. Still, there are tricks like "swallowing the gun"—reducing the charge of armed robbery to unarmed robbery—that are performed for expediency, not for justice.

"Justice delayed is justice denied," is a root principle of common law, but nowadays the right to a speedy trial is so regularly denied that the thought seems antique. Last Aug. 1, a witness was prepared to testify that Cornelius Wright, 18, shot him five times in the chest, stomach and legs. Because of a series of

Reprinted by permission. Tribune Media Services Inc.

mishaps and continuances, Wright has been stewing in the Cook County jail for more than eight months. In fact, Wright's delay is the norm; eight months is the average time between arrest and trial. Continuances have so clogged Chicago's courts that the city's Crime Commission issues a monthly "Ten Most Wanted Dispositions" list in an effort to prod the system.

Trial Delays

Detroit Deputy Police Chief James Bannon believes that trial delays work against the victim. "The judge doesn't see the hysterical, distraught victim. He sees a person who comes into court after several months or years who is totally different. He sees a defendant that bears no relationship to what he appeared to be at the time of the crime. He sits there in a nice three-piece suit and keeps his mouth shut. And the judge doesn't see the shouting, raging animal the victim saw when she was being raped, for example. Both the defendant and victim have lawyers, and that's what the court hears: law. It doesn't hear the guts of the crime."

Procedural concerns can cause delays, and in rare cases defendants' rights can be carried to absurd extremes. California Attorney General George Deumejian tells of Willie Edward Level, who was convicted of beating a Bakersfield College woman student to death with a table leg. Level was informed of his right to remain silent and/or have an attorney present (the *Miranda* ruling). He waived these rights and confessed the murder. Yet the California Court of Appeals threw out the conviction because Level had asked to speak to his mother at the time of his arrest and had not been permitted to; had he been able to do so, it was argued, he might not have made his confession.

"There's nothing in *Miranda* that says a defendant has the right to talk with his mother or a friend," says Deumejian. "It says he can talk to a lawyer or not at all. It's so much of this kind of thing that makes a mockery of the system. And every time you have one of these rulings it has the effect of dragging out the length of cases, which builds in more and more delays. We've got a murder case in Sacramento that's been in the pretrial state for four years."

Add to this the fact that witnesses are discouraged and lost by trial delays. In New York the average number of appearances a witness has to make in a given disposition is 17. Few people have the time or stamina to see a case through.

Bail System

Then there is the matter of bail. In a recent speech before the American Bar Association, Chief Justice Warren Burger argued for tightening the standards for releasing defendants on bail, which seems justifiable. But the subject is complicated. Technically, judges are supposed to base their decisions about bail strictly on the likelihood of a defendant's appearing for trial. In practice, however, this is mere guesswork, and a great many serious crimes are committed by people out on bail or by bail jumpers, who are often given bail when rearrested. One sound reason for a bail system is to avoid locking up anyone before he is proved guilty. But it is simply unrealistic to disregard the criterion of likely dangerousness, even though it raises serious constitutional questions. It has probably resulted in more tragedies than a different standard would result in denials of civil liberties.

Criminals Circumvent Justice

Incredible disparity makes the system a roulette wheel. It depends on where you commit a crime, which judge hears the case and whether you're smart enough to follow the first rule of crime. Commit it with somebody more important than you so that you can turn them in and make a plea bargain for yourself. The net result is that, however tough we may be in theory, the average criminal does not think he's going to do time for serious crimes. Criminals are gamblers by nature. They say to themselves, "If there's any chance that I might get off, I'll probably get off."

Alan M. Dershowitz, *U.S. News & World Report,* August 9, 1982.

Judges blame the cops, and cops blame the judges. Patrick F. Healy, executive director of the Chicago Crime Commission, says judges are plain lazy. "Last year we did a spot check, and the judges' day on the bench totaled 3 hours 49 minutes." The judges will not concede laziness, but several of the nation's best, like Marvin Frankel, former federal judge in the District Court of Manhattan, admit to a "remarkable lack of consistency" in the judiciary. Judge Lois Forer, a most respected criminal-court justice in Philadelphia, contends that it "simply isn't true" that defendants get off on technicalities. It is just that "the system is overloaded." She also emphasizes the problem of sloppy preparations: "It's truly painful when there's someone you're pretty sure committed a crime, and they [police, prosecutors] don't bring in the evidence."

Almost every critic of the system cites the lack of prison space. Despite the enormously high operating costs ($4 billion annually for all U.S. penal institutions), more prison space is an absolute necessity. New York State has between 22,000 and 24,000 jail cells. All are filled, some beyond proper capacity. Twice this year local officials in Missouri were asked not to send any more inmates to the state penitentiary. As a result the St. Louis county jail had to retain seven prisoners who ought to have been in the state pen, even though it meant holding eleven more inmates than the jail was intended to hold. Florida, which already has a higher proportion of its citizenry under lock and key than any other state, may need to spend $83 million on new prison construction and staff. This month 223 supposedly non-violent inmates of Illinois' 13 prisons were given early release to make room for 223 newcomers. New York Police Inspector Richard Dillon, one of the nation's most thoughtful law officers, cites lack of prison space as the primary cause of city crime—the ultimate reason for inappropriate plea bargains, premature paroles, careless bail and too brief sentences.

Juvenile Crime

Finally, the criminal justice system fails at its most sensitive level, that of juvenile crime. Until recently few juvenile courts admitted there was such a thing as a bad boy, restricting their vision of youthful offenders to memories of Father Flanagan's Boys Town or to Judge Tom Clark's quaint view that "every boy, in his heart, would rather steal second base than an automobile." In fact, there are several boys these days who would prefer to kill the umpire, and who have done so, only to receive light sentences or none at all. A study by Marvin Wolfgang at the University of Pennsylvania traced the criminal careers of 10,000 males born in 1948. By the age of 16, 35% had one arrest, but then almost all stopped committing crimes. A small group, however, did not: 627 had five arrests by the time they were adults. They accounted for two-thirds of all the violent crime attributed to the group and almost all the homicides. "This is the group that society is afraid of, and rightly so," says Wolfgang. He is now studying a new group, born in 1958, which is "even nastier and more violent. We should concentrate on them and capture them as soon as possible."

Of course, there is no place to put this hard core, and that is part of the problem. The main difficulty, however, is a Pollyannish, outdated vision of youth, one that results in treating a child not as a potentially responsible human being but rather as some vague romantic entity, capable of continuous regeneration. An underage murderer may be put away for a few months or not at all. As Harvard's James Q. Wilson says, "The adult system is harsh, but before that it's a free ride." The ride is not only free, but clean. At the age of 18, juvenile criminals in many states start all over with unblemished records no matter how many crimes they have committed earlier.

In short, the criminal justice system is not really a system—at least not one in which the individual parts work well on their own or mesh effectively with each other.

"It might be difficult to admit, but in fact we are a society of lawbreakers."

America's Social System Causes Crime

Robert Elias

Robert Elias is assistant professor of political science, chair of the Graduate Program in Public Policy and Citizen Participation, and director/founder of the Peace and Social Justice Program at Tufts University in Massachusetts. His research has appeared in *Victimology*, the *Journal of Social Issues, Social Policy, The Progressive,* and *Citizen Participation.* He is the author of *Victims of the System: Crime Victims and Compensation in American Politics* and *Criminal Justice and The Politics of Victimization: Victims Victimology and Human Rights.* In the following viewpoint, Mr. Elias states that the way to reduce crime is not through justice system reform but rather through a transformation of fundamental social values.

As you read, consider the following questions:

1. What are some of the major "crimes that don't count" with which the author believes we should be concerned?
2. Why are these "crimes" so often not considered when we think of crime?
3. What does the author say we must do to reduce crime?

Robert Elias, "Crimes That Don't Count," *The Progressive,* September 1981. Reprinted by permission from *The Progressive,* 409 East Main Street, Madison, Wisconsin, 53703. Copyright © 1981, The Progressive, Inc.

We've heard it all before: Violence is the work of "professional criminals," a small group of repeat offenders who hold the rest of us hostage. This analysis, of course, constitutes the ageless practice of blaming "bad apples," implying that if we can just put away the few hardened criminals, then the system will be cleansed. In fact, it grossly ignores the real, underlying biases and presumptions of American criminal justice, and, therefore, the real problem.

One of these biases shows up in the way we define violent crime in the first place. We tend to emphasize the crimes of only some Americans—those of the lower and working classes. Some of these acts are, indeed, violent. But our preoccupation with rape, murder, and the other index crimes of the Federal Bureau of Investigation's Uniform Crime Reports diverts our attention from many other acts of violence which are not even talked about, much less made criminal. And yet this latter kind of violence poses a far greater threat to our lives and limbs than the isolated, ugly acts that fit our standard definition of crime.

Consider, for instance, violence in the workplace. Jeffrey Reiman of American University did just that, comparing it with the threat posed by so-called "common crimes." In one year, he wrote in his recent book, *The Rich Get Richer and the Poor Get Prison: Ideology, Class and Criminal Justice*, a liberal estimate of the number of deaths caused by common crimes was 20,000.

Deaths on the Job

This is an alarming and considerable number, but it pales when compared to deaths on the job. Each year, workplace injuries cause 14,200 deaths—almost all of which are preventable by safety devices. In addition, 100,000 people die annually of diseases that can be traced to coal tar, dust, asbestos, and other substances. All of these deaths are also preventable. A death resulting from a common crime may occur every twenty-six minutes in the United States, but a death resulting from a preventable industrial cause occurs every four minutes. Is permitting hazards in the workplace truly a lesser crime than street violence?

Or take health care. Improper emergency care, Reiman writes, kills 20,000 people each year, and unnecessary operations claim 16,000 lives. It has been estimated that 22 per cent of our prescriptions are unnecessary, and improper drug use causes an additional 2,000 to 10,000 deaths every year. This readily competes with our 3,600 annual stabbing deaths. Should we add the scalpel to our list of lethal weapons? How about the syringe, or the prescription?

Moreover, about 350,000 people die yearly of cancer, and scientists now tell us that between 60 and 90 per cent of those cases result from preventable, environmental sources such as chemicals. In his book, Reiman argues that although ending this kind of violence would be expensive, we would hardly claim that it was too expensive to fight a foreign invader that killed 1,000 people a day and that would kill, over the years, one out of every four Americans.

Ignored Violence

Examples of ignored violence abound in our society. So why has it not been defined as crime? One response could be that while work place hazards and prescription drugs may produce violence and death, they are not intended to do so. In fact, however, the vast majority of violent, common crimes are not premeditated; they are committed in moments of anger or fear. On the other hand, a mine owner acts with great forethought in sending workers underground each day without first installing safety devices that could avert death and injury. Yet the irrational act is deemed a crime, while the mine owner is thought to be using good business sense.

The truth is that we have been taught to think of crime in the most narrow terms—terms that conveniently exclude the activities of our society's most powerful people.

Punishment of the Underprivileged

In America, the need for vengeance and the ritual of punishment have historically focused on the lower classes. And because the criminal justice system is so thoroughly intertwined with the political system, the courts are selective in meting out punishment. For the most part, those least capable of rising above their poverty or ignorance are the ones who are punished. The underprivileged can react only with rage at the brutal circumstances of their captivity.

Michael Specter, *The Nation,* March 13, 1983.

The same bias that defines what is criminal in the first place determines how the law will be applied, and so middle and upper classes are far less subject to arrest, conviction, and punishment. Yet studies have shown that *lawbreaking* is, in fact, epidemic in all classes; there are no statistical differences in the rates of criminality among rich and poor, although it is arguable that the latter surely have far greater reason to commit crimes. It might be difficult to admit, but in fact we are a society of lawbreakers.

Real Cause of Crime

What causes our extensive lawlessness? *Time* magazine, in its analysis, gave a token nod to the "social ills of poverty, ignorance, racism, and the disintegration of the family," but placed full blame on the criminal justice system, as if crime were merely an administrative problem. In fact, unremitting and extensive poverty and racism really are sources of crime, and in economically strained times, more crimes are committed. If you are poor, and have little access to the more sophisticated means of stealing money to survive—or to pay for drugs which the upper classes can afford on their paychecks and even, in some cases, purchase legally—you will resort to violent and illegal ones. Crime is an accommodation by some to the economic realities of our society.

What, then, explains crime among the rich? Business competition, for one thing, gives an air of legitimacy to shady deals made in the name of maintaining profit margins. Even without pressing economic incentive, many people are alienated by our large and oppressive social institutions. Surely, they think, a little loss will not hurt a supermarket chain or department store. It is easier to rip off a stranger, especially if the stranger is not even a person.

Finally, we have created a society that is alienating for rich *and* poor, plutocrat *and* pauper. Unable to cope with demands that we succeed and consume at high levels, we vent our frustration in crime, often violent crime.

The way, then, to reduce the level of crime in our society is not through reform of juvenile justice systems, police-community relations, or sentencing practices; nor is it through building more prisons and putting more people in them. What we need to do is make fundamental, systemic changes that diminish or abolish unrestrained competition, community and family fragmentation, alienation, and inequality. These are the major sources of crime in America, and they produce lawbreaking at all levels.

Do we make these fundamental transformations, or do we live with our cliches, failed reforms, and likely a knife—or scalpel—at our throats?

Recognizing Stereotypes

A stereotype is an oversimplified or exaggerated description of people or things. Stereotyping can be favorable. However, most stereotyping tends to be highly uncomplimentary and, at times, degrading.

Stereotyping grows out of our prejudices. When we stereotype someone, we are prejudging him or her. Consider the following example: Mr. X is convinced that all Mexicans are lazy, sloppy and careless people. The Diaz family, a family of Mexicans, happen to be his next-door neighbors. One evening, upon returning home from work, Mr. X notices that the garbage pails in the Diaz driveway are overturned and that the rubbish is scattered throughout the driveway. He immediately says to himself: "Isn't that just like those lazy, sloppy and careless Mexicans?" The possibility that a group of neighborhood vandals or a pack of stray dogs may be responsible for the mess never enters his mind. Why not? Simply because he has prejudged all Mexicans and will keep his stereotype consistent with his prejudice. The famous (or infamous) Archie Bunker of television fame is a classic example of our Mr. X.

The following statements relate to the subject matter in this chapter. Consider each statement carefully. *Mark S for any statement that is an example of stereotyping. Mark N for any statement that is not an example of stereotyping. Mark U if you are undecided about any statement.*

If you are doing this activity as a member of a class or group, compare your answers with those of other class or group members. Be able to defend you answers. You may discover that others will come to different conclusions than you. Listening to the reasons others present for their answers may give you valuable insights in recognizing stereotypes.

If you are reading this book alone, ask others if they agree with your answers. You too will find this interaction very valuable.

S = *stereotype*
N = *not a stereotype*
U = *undecided*

1. Criminals are primarily poor people on welfare who want to supplement their monthly welfare check.

2. Career criminals can be recognized by certain facial characteristics such as a long nose, small eyes, and bony cheekbones.

3. Juvenile delinquents usually come from homes where the mother has an outside job.

4. Teenagers commit more property crimes than any other age group because they have not yet found a socially acceptable way to vent their anger.

5. Most criminals come from families of criminals where crime is a way of life.

6. America's poor are likely to be honest and law-abiding citizens.

7. Criminals are nearly always Black or Hispanic.

8. Most members of minority races are productive members of American society.

9. Criminals of a minority race most often prey on white people to show their anger at an unjust society.

10. Many criminals go free because judges and police officers are corrupt.

11. As criminals age, most eventually go straight.

12. Respectable people who live in nice areas and are involved in community activities are not a cause of crime in America.

13. Poor people are more often victims of crime than are wealthy people.

14. The overwhelming causes of crime are lenient judges and ineffective police operations.

15. Parents who do not "spare the rod and spoil the child" are less apt to produce juvenile delinquents.

Bibliography

The following list of periodical articles deals with the subject matter of this chapter.

Charles Colson   "Taking a Stand When Law and Justice Conflict," *Christianity Today*, February 4, 1983.

Cristie Davies   "Some Causes of Crime," *Current* March 4, 1983.

David Gibson   "Reforming the Criminal Justice System," *Origins*, February 17, 1983.

Bruce T. Grindal   "The Thrill of Crime: Busting Loose," *The Humanist*, January-February 1982.

Charles Gould   "Crime Marches On: Swift and Sure Punishment for Law Breakers," *Vital Speeches of the Day*, January 15, 1982.

Ernest van den Haag   "Thinking About Crime Again," *Commentary*, December 1983.

W. Herbert   "The Case of the Missing Hormone," *Science News*, October 30, 1982.

John A. Howard   "A Different View of Crime and What to Do About It," *Vital Speeches of the Day*, March 1, 1983.

Thomas J. McGrew   "Cracks in the Wall," *Inquiry*, September 1983.

Origins   "Reforming the Criminal Justice System," February 17, 1983.

Richard Pollack   "The Epilepsy Defense," *Atlantic Monthly*, May 1984.

Gerald Parshall   "American Justice," *U.S. News & World Report*, November 1, 1982.

Thomas J. Reese   "Demythologizing Crime," *America*, March 24, 1984.

Time   "Street Sentence: Vigilante Justice in Buffalo," August 15, 1983.

Frank Trippett   "A Red Light for Scofflaws," *Time*, January 24, 1983.

James Q. Wilson   "Thinking About Crime," *The Atlantic Monthly*, September 1983.

CHAPTER 2

How Should Criminals Be Treated?

"Revisions in sentencing policy have begun to stress the role of imprisonment in simply punishing offenders and keeping them off the streets."

Harsh Sentences Are Effective Punishment

Peter W. Greenwood

Peter W. Greenwood is an educator on criminology and has served on the faculties of the California Institute of Technology, the Air Force Institute of Technology, and the Rand Graduate Institute. He is president of the Association for Criminal Justice Research and is presently directing studies on California's juvenile justice system for the California Assembly. Mr. Greenwood's most recent book is *Selective Incapacitation*. In the following viewpoint, he explains the three methods in which he believes imprisonment of criminals can best benefit society.

As you read, consider the following questions:

1. What are the three basic means by which incarceration affects crime rates?
2. How does the author think that deterrence theory conflicts with theories of rehabilitation?
3. According to the author, how does the crime rate of individual inmates relate to the incapacitation effects of imprisonment?

"Controlling the Crime Rate through Imprisonment," by Peter W. Greenwood, in *Crime and Public Policy* edited by James Q. Wilson. Copyright © Institute for Contemporary Studies, 1983, San Francisco.

With respect to the use of imprisonment, the American criminal justice system is at an important crossroads. At the same time that a dissatisfied public is pressing vociferously for greater protection against violent crime and prisons are overflowing with new inmates, the concepts on which we formerly based our decisions about the sentencing and release of offenders have undergone a major revision. Most of the existing sentencing laws in the U.S. were written at a time when a principal goal of imprisonment was thought to be rehabilitation. In recent years, however, a growing body of research has questioned the efficacy of rehabilitation programs and called attention to the inequities produced by sentencing policies based on this goal. As a result, the emphasis on rehabilitation has been largely set aside, and the latest revisions in sentencing policy have begun to stress the role of imprisonment in simply punishing offenders and keeping them off the streets. The most conspicuous consequence of this shift has been the unprecedented growth of the number of offenders going to prison.

Yet the question remains: given the limited resources of the system, how can we best use imprisonment to contribute to the control of crime?. . .

There are three basic means through which incarceration can affect future crime rates: (1) the incarceration experience can change the propensity of those incarcerated to engage in crime when they are released; (2) the threat of incarceration can deter potential offenders from engaging in crime; and (3) incarceration prevents those crimes that would have been committed by inmates during their period of incarceration.

Rehabilitation

Prison may reduce the tendency of an offender to commit further crimes through either rehabilitation or what is termed "special deterrence." It is also possible that criminal propensities of some offenders will be intensified by prison experiences, either because inmates, having been labeled as criminals, will come to behave as such; because prisons are "schools for crime"; or because long periods of incarceration may inhibit an inmate from learning to function in an open society. Whatever the cause, the basic measure of the outcome is the recidivism rate.

For most of the past century, the criminal justice system attempted to control the crime problem through efforts at rehabilitation. Research and experimental programs were focused on developing improved methods for diagnosing the underlying problems that led to an offender's criminal behavior and developing programs that could respond to those problems. Probation, presentence investigation reports, reception clinics in prison, indeterminate sentences, and parole services are all legacies of this faith in the rehabilitation ideal.

By the 1970s, the picture had changed considerably. None of the numerous approaches to rehabilitation tested during the preceding decade was found to produce consistently significant reductions in recidivism rates, particularly for the more serious offenders. The view that "nothing works" has since become the conventional wisdom among most corrections practitioners and researchers. It is now universally recognized that a substantial number of inmates will not recidivate after their release, but there is little faith that the size of this fraction can be increased by rehabilitation programs. Whatever residual hope remains for rehabilitation is focused on juveniles and the least sophisticated adult criminals.

Vengeance Makes Punishment Intelligible

The element of retribution—vengeance, if you will—does not make punishment cruel and unusual, it makes punishment intelligible. It distinguishes punishment from therapy. Rehabilitation may be an ancillary result of punishment, but we punish to serve justice, by giving people what they deserve.

George F. Will, *Newsweek*, May 24, 1982.

The same research tends to contradict the claim that prisons intensify criminal behavior. There is no compelling evidence that incarceration either extends the length of the criminal career or leads to increases in crime severity. In all likelihood, imprisonment has a positive effect on some inmates and a negative impact on others, with the two effects canceling each other out. Until a way is found of predicting in which category any given offender falls, a prediction that many practitioners continually attempt to make—apparently in most cases unsuccessfully—neither rehabilitation nor special deterrence effects can provide a useful basis for sentencing decisions.

Deterrence

Although general deterrence has historically been recognized as a major objective of the criminal justice system, it is only in the past twenty years that researchers have begun to explore its effect in detail. At its simplest level, deterrence theory holds that criminal behavior is influenced by the same types of cost/benefit incentives as any other type of economic activity. As the costs or risks associated with a particular type of crime are increased, the attractiveness of that type of crime to potential offenders should decrease. As a matter of public policy, the cost of engaging in crime can be increased by increasing the probability of apprehension, conviction, and incarceration, or by increasing the length of terms.

There is little disagreement that the criminal justice system does deter many would-be offenders. Debates about the impact of deterrence are concerned with the effects of marginal changes in sentencing patterns on particular types of offenders. For instance, there is considerable disagreement about the ways in which risks are communicated to offenders. Do they respond to the language of a statute or to the ways in which it is applied? If a law is passed requiring a prison term for every defendant who is convicted of residential burglary, does it matter whether the law is strictly applied or whether a number of defendants are allowed to plead guilty to lesser counts? There is considerable debate about the relationship between the severity of sanctions and the certainty with which they are applied. Will longer sentences for robbery deter potential offenders if fewer than 5 out of 100 robberies result in conviction? Should more offenders be sentenced to prison for shorter periods of time? There is also debate about how sanctions may affect offenders differentially, at different points in their career. Some would argue that young, unsophisticated offenders, who are not yet fully committed to a criminal way of life, are the ones who are most easily deterred by sanctions. Yet this view directly contradicts those who argue that criminal processing only reinforces the criminal identity of these marginal offenders by labeling them as criminal, and that they should be diverted out of the criminal justice system to be treated by community-based programs.

Unfortunately, empirical studies have done little to resolve most of these disputes. Quasi-experimental studies, which attempt to measure the impact of changes in sanction severity over time, and cross-sectional studies, which compare crime rates across jurisdictions that differ in their sanction severity, are both plagued by a number of methodological difficulties. A recent review of these studies by a panel established by the National Academy of Sciences concluded that while the findings of the research are generally consistent with the deterrence hypothesis—i.e., jurisdictions with high sanctions generally have lower rates of crime—the data do not prove the existence of deterrence effects or indicate their magnitude.

Of course, criminal justice officials do not have the luxury of postponing sentencing decisions until the final evidence on deterrence questions is in. Officials must establish or support sentencing policies that, in effect conform to or depart from deterrence theory. For instance, deterrence studies suggest that the marginal impact of changes in certainty is more important than the effect of changes in severity. If a jurisdiction convicts, on the average, about 1,000 robbery defendants per year, this finding would argue that sending 1,000 defendants to prison for one year would deter more crimes than sending only 500 to prison for two years—the kind of policy now followed in most jurisdictions. Thus deterrence theory turns out to produce policy guidance that is in direct conflict with theories of rehabilitation or incapacitation, both of which would focus resources on those offenders thought to represent the greatest risk to society.

Incapacitation and Crime Rates

The third method through which incarceration can affect crime rates is called incapacitation. For any offenders who would have continued to commit crimes after their conviction, incarceration prevents the crimes they would have committed during their period of confinement. The amount of crime prevented by incapacitation is obviously directly related to the rate at which inmates would have commited crimes if they were free. The higher the crime rates of individual inmates, the greater the incapacitation effects of any given period of imprisonment.

But this general observation must be qualified. Incapacitation effects will occur only if the period of incarceration is subtracted from the total length of a criminal's career. If a one-year sentence simply extends an offender's career by one year, then the incapacitation effects are zero; his crimes are merely postponed.

"There are many legitimate ways to help lift the burden of crime from taxpayers' shoulders, while still punishing the guilty."

Harsh Sentences Are Counterproductive

Jean Harris

Jean Harris graduated magna cum laude in economics from Smith College and was headmistress at Madeira School, a girls preparatory school in Michigan. She is currently serving a prison sentence for the murder of her former lover, Dr. Herman Tarnower, author of the famous *Scarsdale Diet*. (During her trial, however, she argued convincingly that his death was accidental.) The following viewpoint appeared in an article she authored since her imprisonment in which she describes three types of alternative sentencing of criminals that she believes would effectively reduce the crime and recidivism rates.

As you read, consider the following questions:

1. According to the author, what effect does prison have on the imprisoned?
2. Why does the author feel that some of her fellow inmates should not be incarcerated?
3. What three alternatives to prison did the author suggest?

Jean Harris, "Inside Story," *New York*, June 13, 1983. Reprinted with permission of the author.

"Come at me, Harris!" the woman said. "Come at me! Wanna hit me, Harris? Why 'ncha hit me? Hit me here!" The woman was a correction officer at Bedford Hills Correctional Facility, and I was being "corrected," at society's expense. For months, this woman—who earns more than many good teachers—had been trying to get me to hit her so she could charge me with assault and have me sent to segregation. She'd just finished strip-searching me following a meeting with friends in the visiting room. . . .Her specialty is "squats," and that day she outdid herself. "That ain't a good squat. Squat again, and this time cough. Cough harder." Finally, under her goading I started to shriek and howl and shake, until people came from all around and tried to quiet me. That day, I thought I could never go through it again and remain sane. I was wrong. I am still reasonably sane, and I went through it many more times before the woman was finally removed—not fired but transferred to another facility, where she now helps to "correct" other unfortunates.

My point in describing the "squat lady" is not to shock or arouse pity but to raise questions about a growing part of society's tax bill—the part that goes to pay for prisons. Are taxpayers getting their money's worth? The people of New York spend over $3 billion a year on the many-headed monster called the criminal-justice system. Nearly half a billion goes for prisons alone. The cost of keeping one prisoner for one year is about $20,000—for far less than that the state could send the inmate to Smith.

This money is being spent at a time when essential social programs are being canceled, thousands of New Yorkers are homeless, old people are afraid they'll live longer than they can afford, and school budgets are being dangerously shortchanged. According to the Ford Foundation, 64 million Americans—28 out of every 100—are functionally illiterate. Many of these people are doomed to fail unless they can be educated. But education is competing for the same dollars as corrections—and corrections is clearly a growth industry. . . .

A Place Called Bedlam

Bedford can't always find room in the reception area for arriving inmates, so newcomers get jammed into any available space—the medical unit, for example, or even the protective custody unit, a section of the prison that's part of the segregation building, where the inmates with the most serious behavior problems are held. Some women in segregation are more mentally ill than criminal. They cry all night, scream obscenities, set their beds on fire, throw feces on the guards and on one another, and generally behave as if the place were Bedlam, not Bedford.

I spoke recently with a young woman who had spent the first week of her stay at Bedford in protective custody. Her eyes were still wide with fright. "This isn't prison, it's a crazy house," she said. Prison administrations—even enlightened ones, as here at Bedford—have no control over the number of inmates sent to them. Bodies are delivered, and a place must be found for them.

As more and more prisoners are packed into existing facilities, the opportunity to work and take part in rehabilitation programs declines. At Attica, more than 500 men have no jobs to go to, and spend 20 to 23 hours a day locked in 50-square-foot cells. They get little exercise, no job training, no education, and virtually no responsibility. Recidivism is born of this kind of costly neglect. The average prison inmate is about 27 years old, with an active sexual drive, and cut off from legitimate avenues of sex. The constant ferment of prison life isn't hard to understand. . . .

Incarceration Costs

Despite their love of incarceration, Americans do not want to pay the price of locking up so many citizens. It costs at least $50,000 to build a cell these days, and to keep a prisoner in a cell requires another $1,000 to $2,000 a month. We need a solution to the dilemma that surfaces whenever someone (usually an economist) notes that as the state increases the cost of crime for criminals (longer and harsher prison terms for more offenders), it increases its own economic costs proportionately because it must build, man, and maintain new prisons, pay board-and-room costs of prisoners for longer terms, and pay for increased police and court work as well.

Donald R. Cressey, *Society*, July/August 1982.

Motivation almost vanishes in prison. Getting to work on time, for example, is never applauded—and it's sometimes made impossible. Every day for two years, I have spent time waiting at as many as 76 locked doors: 18 doors to and from meals, 24 to and from work, 8 to and from medication, 12 to and from a visit, and 14 to and from my volunteer job on Fridays. I began knitting mittens during those waits to help salve the utter frustration that comes with throwing away time needlessly. By now, I have knitted more than a hundred pairs. If every door were opened in a minute—and it usually takes longer than that—the time spent standing in front of a locked door would still add up to more than six hours per week, or thirteen days per year. Is that preparation to face the world with drive, energy, and a new attitude? Or is that the sort of thing that creates an embittered, uninterested zombie? One fights to stay whole in prison.

The people opening and closing those doors (it seems to be their principal activity) aren't known as "guards." The law insists that they be called "correction officers"—which has to rank among the state's most blatant hypocrisies, considering their style of correcting. These officers receive minimal training, often only a few weeks, though their own union says that sixteen weeks of training should be required. To be fair, there are some correction officers who live up to the title—decent people with sound values, good judgement, self-respect, and common sense. But there aren't enough of them. Twice I've seen new C.O.'s ask an inmate to come to the officer's station to show how to open and close the cell doors. I've tried with other inmates to hold down a prisoner having a seizure, to keep her from pounding her head open on the floor and swallowing her tongue, while a C.O. stood by, hands on hips, and said, "She just does that to get attention." I've heard someone shout "Fire!" and seen the C.O. panic and lock all the doors, with inmates inside.

An Arsonist with Matches

The day an inmate in the cell next to mine set her bed on fire, a C.O. immediately locked her cell, and the inmate sat happily on her toilet, watching the fire burn closer. It took screams from other inmates to get the door open, and it was inmates who ran in and pulled her out. The woman is in prison for arson, she is mentally confused, and three times during the previous night a C.O. had brought her matches "because she asked for them."

The same woman will be released in the next few months, "if I can find a place to stay when I go out." Mentally ill and without money, marketable skills, family help, or friends, she spends her days writing sad, rather lovely poetry. If she is let out, almost as surely as the morning follows the night she will return someday to prison, unless she dies first. Is prison the place she should be?

The nature of prison life seems to be written into the rules of medical care. The seriously ill are sometimes overlooked, while the doctors' and nurses' time is wasted on nonsense. I had to make an appointment and get written permission from the doctor to wear a flimsy little pantie girdle. The reason? "Well, you know, if a woman is pregnant, it isn't good to wear a tight girdle." I'm 60 years old, and a nurse said this to me with a straight face. I had to go to the doctor to get a "prescription" for a one-a-day vitamin pill, and the doctor told me, in his most pontifical tone, "I cannot prescribe a one-a-day vitamin for you until you are examined and have blood tests." Should I have cared? Though I was supplying the girdle and the vitamins, I wasn't paying for the doctor's time or for the tests—the state was.

Taxpayers pay when harm is done—when a prisoner is injured or the law is ignored. Six years ago, inmates won a class-action

By permission of Johnny Hart and News Group, Chicago, Inc.

suit against Bedford, challenging the medical procedures then in effect. Two years ago, they won $125,000 in a suit over disciplinary proceedings at the prison. Both cases dragged on for years, running up legal fees for the state. But today the risk of a lawsuit doesn't seem to frighten C.O.'s and middle management at all. "Go ahead and sue. It ain't my money" is a familiar comment. . . .

Burden of Crime

There are many legitimate ways to help lift the burden of crime from taxpayers' shoulders, while still punishing the guilty and even making some restitution to victims—something that prison doesn't accommodate. Even if society has given up trying to improve criminals, there's no reason to work at making them worse. Immediate steps can be taken to reduce the cost of prison without increasing the risk to society.

One such step was recently taken at Bedford Hills, with the opening of Fiske Cottage, an honor house for 26 inmates—myself among them. Fiske was built almost 70 years ago as a separate building at Westfield Farms, a women's facility that was Bedford's predecessor. When the law was changed to require that each locked cell contain running water and a toilet, Fiske was closed down. It had been shuttered for fifteen years when the new Bedford administration, headed by Superintendent Frank R. Headley, decided to make use of it. Installing plumbing in each room would have been exorbitantly expensive, but Headley took another approach: He turned it into an honor cottage in which none of the rooms is locked. Total renovation, including the installation of a new heating system and the addition of prison-made furniture, cost $44,000. Building 26 cells would have cost more than $2 million. Of course, in addition to a reasonable price, Fiske has another, immeasurable benefit: 26 women have been given the opportunity to prove that they can govern themselves and make intelligent decisions. . . .

Prison Alternatives

The surest way to avoid prison waste is to release some prisoners sooner, or not to put them there in the first place. Work-release programs are probably the most constructive alternative to too much caging. No program better eases the transition from inside to outside. . . .

Intensive probation for nonviolent first offenders is another good alternative to prison. Under that system, the offender remains out of prison, under close supervision. He or she may be independently employed, or may be working in the community to make restitution. In some instances, weekends are spent in prison for a certain number of months. Mothers are allowed to stay with their children, thus eliminating the added expense of foster-care services. . . .

Parole violators are another group filling too many top-security cells. They are people who have been released and have not committed new crimes but have failed to adhere to the strict rules that parole properly lays down. A parolee may be returned to prison for getting drunk and disorderly, for using drugs, for being seen with the wrong people (though usually "the wrong people" are the only friends an ex-prisoner has), for getting married without the parole officer's consent, or even for getting pregnant. . . .

Plea Bargaining

There is one short-term saving—at long-term expense—that the public should also look at when assessing the costs of the criminal-justice system. It's called plea bargaining. Americans are proud of the jury system in this country, but 85 to 90 percent of the people in prison did not go to trial. They pleaded guilty to a lesser crime than the one they had been charged with and ar-ranged for a lighter sentence. Thus is revolving-door justice created. And what about the innocent, and those untutored in "jail-house smarts"? They put years of their lives on the line and go to trial. I know rather well three women who were urged to plea-bargain: Two were offered probation, and one was offered "one to three." All professed their innocence and insisted on a trial. All three were found guilty by their juries and sentenced to fifteen years to life in prison. One of them was granted clemency last year after serving almost five years. The other two are still here, and there are more than a few other women like them. If it is safe and just for a person to be given probation and sent back into the world, by what standards of human decency can you cage the person for fifteen years? The one unforgiveable error in the criminal-justice system is to be innocent. Young Americans are taught that trial by jury is a right, freely given, but that is not so. It is enormously expensive for the innocent, and casually sidestepped by the guilty. Plea bargaining with career criminals is false economy, but one of the few economies the system prac-tices enthusiastically.

Americans As "Good Guys"

America is a violent and crime-ridden country. There are more homicides per year in New York City than in France and Britain combined. Yet most Americans live out their lives believing the myth that they are the good guys. American prison sentences are the longest in the Western World, and only South Africa and the Soviet Union have more prisoners per 100,000 people than the United States does.

Incarceration is a violent act. Violence is a response to violence, but not a solution to it. The hypocrisy that mas-querades as criminal justice has done little to make the country safer, to compensate crime victims, or to prepare wrongdoers to re-enter the community. The system clearly doesn't work, and it costs a fortune—two of the best possible arguments for change.

"To pronounce correctional. . .treatment a failure. . .will only result in a more intensive application of a losing punitive strategy."

Rehabilitation Can Work

Michael J. Lillyquist

Michael J. Lillyquist is currently a fulltime writer in Tuscon, Arizona. Prior to 1981, he taught criminal psychology for twelve years at the University of Wisconsin at Platteville, and authored a textbook entitled *Undertaking and Changing Criminal Behavior*. Mr. Lillyquist has a Ph.D. in social psychology from the University of Arizona and is working on a new book entitled *Who Needs Crime*. In following viewpoint, he cites factors that he is certain delude the public into believing that rehabilitation is ineffective.

As you read, consider the following questions:

1. Does the author think that 'scaring people straight' is effective? Do you agree?
2. What are the five reasons the author gives for why success in rehabilitation is not apparent to the public?
3. How does the United States incarceration rate compare to the rest of the world?

Michael J. Lillyquist, "We Need to Admit That Treatment Can Work," *Corrections*, February 1981. Reprinted with permission of Criminal Justice Publications.

The darkest hour for those who would change criminal behavior using something other than naked force came in 1974. Robert Martinson, now deceased, announced that the extensive evaluation research that he and his colleagues had undertaken indicated that the various approaches to the rehabilitation of criminals, both in prison and in community corrections programs, had shown meager results. This conclusion was readily accepted by politicians, political scientists, sociologists and editorial writers of all persuasions. Our "soft" approach to intervention had been tried and was found wanting. Now that efforts at rehabilitation (and social change as well) had been shown to be ineffective, we could get back to the old business of punishment and incapacitation.

This conclusion was incredible, though the fact dawned slowly for some, and for some not at all. Was it possible that all attempts to change individuals or crime-producing social conditions had failed in all cases?. . . .

For lack of alternatives, we feel forced to resort to "scaring people straight," as in New Jersey's delinquency prevention program at Rahway state prison. Showing how horrifying prison existence can be is expected to make kids think twice before they make themselves candidates for such abuse. Whether this is effective or not, it illustrates a chilling point: The efforts of prison reformers are being blunted; we *want* prisons to be horrible so that those of us fortunate enough to be on the outside will try to stay here. But what of those inside? A distasteful image of human sacrifice emerges: Inmates are brutalized and thus lost to society to teach *us* a lesson. (Perhaps, using similar logic, we should discontinue attempts to alleviate the suffering of victims of lung cancer, the better to deter smoking.) No one supposes that prisoners are being helped by such dehumanization. But, we are told, the other approaches have failed. It's not that we didn't try. . . .

No Simple Solutions

Perhaps we should try again. If we will give up our search for simple solutions—such as the ideal treatment program that cures all criminal behavior—more effective programs will emerge. Person-centered and situation-centered research on prison and community treatment programs are simplistic, and the conclusions of these studies could have been foreseen without ever undertaking them. The more sophisticated research question is this: What kinds of people respond most favorably to what types of treatment programs? The "interactionist" approach that considers both the person and the situation at the same time yields encouraging answers. Some people do benefit from treatment programs, but not equally from all types. And some programs are effective, though not with all kinds of people. The trick is to predict, at some early point, who will benefit most in what type of program.

When the question is posed this way, successes emerge from unexpected places—sometimes out of the ashes of supposed failures. For example, Stuart Adams found that inmates in a study of his did not, as a whole, benefit from individual psychotherapy. Those receiving psychotherapy were rearrested at a rate comparable to control groups following release. But when inmates, upon arrival at prison, were differentiated into an amenable group (thought to be able to benefit from psychotherapy), and a nonamenable group (judged likely not to benefit from such therapy), an interesting interaction appeared: Amenables did better than the controls receiving no such therapy, while nonamenables actually did worse than controls. This two-category classification yielded recommendations as to which people should be given the therapy, and, just as importantly, from which people this particular treatment should be withheld.

Jails Teach Criminal Behavior

Instead of making a criminal offender pay for damages suffered by victims, we tax the victim and other law-abiding citizens to raise money to "keep" the offender in costly quarters. Rather than putting the offender into a productive role, we store him in a warehouse called prison. And despite your good efforts, we generally provide insufficient basic education, training in vocational skills, and instruction in human values. Instead, we expose offenders to schooling in more deleterious criminal behavior.

Mark W. Cannon, *Vital Speeches of the Day,* October 1, 1982.

Numerous other interactions have been found: that delinquent youths with strong self-discipline fare better in an unrestrictive setting than do those with weaker controls; that neurotic or conflicted offenders respond better to individual counseling; that manipulative youths respond better to a transactional analysis program than to behavior modification. The person administering the treatment makes a difference. Parole officers judged adequate in the performance of their duties have greater success with small case loads. Conversely, inadequate parole officers are less ineffective with large case loads. Apparently their bungling is diluted by the large numbers.

Those who believe that harsh penalties must again be exacted of criminals because treatment has failed are wrong on two counts. First, longer sentences do not result in improved recidivism rates. (For those inmates who are the best risks, longer prison sentences are especially harmful, increasing the likelihood of recidivism.) Second, treatment has *not* failed. Successes abound, though even the most optimistic treatment personnel acknowledge the decay of rehabilitative success over time unless steps are taken to change the environment that contributed to the criminal act in the first place. Those who are so certain that less punitive approaches have failed perhaps speak more clearly about themselves than about the treatment programs.

A Need to Fail

Federal Bureau of Investigation statistics reveal that about one-third of released inmates are reincarcerated for a new offense. Other ex-inmates, of course, are arrested but not convicted, and still others return to prison for a violation of the conditions of parole and not for the commission of a new offense. Why do we hear so frequently that the recidivism rate of those who are imprisoned is between 70 and 80 percent? (In fact, those who use such numbers have confused the percentage of prior imprisonments among current inmates with the percentage of reimprisonments after release.) The frequent citation of figures so wide of the mark must be fulfilling some needs. Do we want our correctional interventions to fail? I think there are several reasons that we do not seek or expect success in this realm:

1) It has been suggested that prisons only succeed by their failures. Most of us, no matter what our occupation, want to be involved in a growth industry, and successful treatment programs might impede an expansion of the prison "business." Similarly, the police officer, judge, criminologist and others of us who work in the criminal justice field would have to find new work were our efforts successful.

2) On an equally cynical note, a society may need a class of people against whom it is socially acceptable to vent aggression. The extremely vitriolic attacks leveled against criminals, and the exceedingly negative stereotypes many hold of the criminal, may serve to displace hostility that we cannot appropriately express toward bosses, spouses and friends. Frustrations with amorphous villains like "the economy" can be directed toward corporeal villains—criminals.

3) We have a pronounced tendency in the United States to make personal attributions for crime, to hold the criminal *personally* responsible for his or her offense. The environmental contributors are thus minimized. If criminal behavior has its source in something deep, personal, and enduring, we can hardly expect much change. If the person *is* a criminal—a personal attribution—we may be more likely to expect that he or she will remain a criminal.

4) Holding something other than the criminal responsible for the crime—an environmental attribution—might implicate ourselves. Painful soul-searching might reveal that *we* are part of the problem. It is easier to believe that we have tried to change the offender and have failed.

5) Finally, inmates themselves may be the last to acknowledge any benefit acquired through prison experience. To do so would be to collaborate with those who denied them their freedom and perhaps their dignity. It would also be an admission that the inmate was in need of some "correcting," a position he or she may be reluctant to take.

Changing Attitudes

So, for a variety of reasons, we may not desire nor want to acknowledge success in changing criminal behavior. As can be seen, changing the attitudes and behavior of the public—the audience for the crime and punishment drama—may be a prerequisite to effective crime control.

Will we continue to build more prisons, give longer sentences, and exact the ultimate punishment? The United States already has an imprisonment rate (including local jails) of 215 per 100,000 population, one of the highest in the world. And with the exception of political prisoners in some totalitarian countries, our inmates serve the longest sentences. Though we believe we are soft on crime, the rest of the world sees us otherwise. To pronounce correctional treatment, within and outside prison, a failure, to preclude a second serious look at treatment techniques, will only result in a more intensive application of a losing punitive strategy. To continue to ask the difficult questions, to classify offenders and offer differential treatment, will be more effective. Coupled with an appreciation of the factors external to the offender that result in criminal behavior along with continued efforts to ameliorate those conditions, "treatment" may soon be removed from the lexicon of retired catchwords. If it is, it will not be hailed as the panacea once believed, but rather will represent a wide variety of practices differentially effective with different individuals.

*"We have an unpleasant method—
deterrence—that works, and a pleasant
method—rehabilitation—that (at least so far)
never has worked."*

Rehabilitation Cannot Work

Gordon Tullock

Gordon Tullock is an educator with a J.D. from the University of Chicago. He is editorial director for the Center for the Study of Public Choice and the author of numerous books including *The Logic of the Law, The Social Dilemma,* and *Trials on Trial.* In the following viewpoint, Mr. Tullock explains his theory that rehabilitation programs are instigated primarily to soften society's punishment of criminals. He states that if criminals know they face rehabilitation rather than punishment, the deterrent effect of incarceration is lost.

As you read, consider the following questions:

1. What are three arguments for punishment of criminals?
2. How does Mr. Tullock believe that punishment and crime are interrelated?
3. Why does the author think that the idea of rehabilitation became so popular in the late 19th century?

Gordon Tullock, "Does Punishment Deter Crime?" Reprinted with permission of Gordon Tullock from *The Public Interest,* Summer 1974.

Traditionally there have been three arguments for the punishment of criminals. The first of these is that punishment is morally required or, another way of putting the same thing, that it is necessary for the community to feel morally satisfied. I will not discuss this further. The two remaining explanations are that punishment deters crime and that it may rehabilitate the criminal. The rehabilitation argument was little used before about 1800, presumably because the punishments in vogue up to that time had little prospect of producing any positive effect upon the moral character of the criminal.

But with the turn to imprisonment as the principal form of punishment—a movement which occurred in the latter part of the 18th and early part of the 19th century—the idea that the prison might "rehabilitate" the prisoner became more common. The word "penitentiary" was coined with the intent of describing a place where the prisoner has the time and the opportunity to repent of his sins and resolve to follow a more socially approved course of action after his release. The idea that prisons would rehabilitate the criminal and that this was their primary purpose gradually replaced the concept of deterrence as the principal publicly announced justification for the punishment system. I should like to defer discussing my views as to why this occurred until the latter part of this article, but here I should like to point out that, whatever the motive or the reason for this change, it certainly was not the result of careful scientific investigation. . . .

Punishment Deters Crime

Most economists who give serious thought to the problem of crime immediately come to the conclusion that punishment will indeed deter crime. The reason is perfectly simple: Demand curves slope downward. If you increase the cost of something, less will be consumed. Thus, if you increase the cost of committing a crime, there will be fewer crimes. The elasticity of the demand curve, of course, might be low, in which case the effect might be small; but there should be at least some effect.

Economists, of course, would not deny that there are other factors that affect the total number of crimes. Unemployment, for example, quite regularly raises the amount of crime and, at least under modern conditions, changes in the age composition of the population seem to be closely tied to changes in the crime rate. The punishment variable, however, has the unique characteristic of being fairly easy to change by government action. Thus, if it does have an effect, we should take advantage of that fact. . . .

In discussing the concept of deterrence, I find that a great many people seem to feel that, although it would no doubt work

"OKAY, SO SECURITY IS A BIT LOOSE. LOOK AT THE PROGRESS WE'VE MADE ON THE OVERCROWDING PROBLEM! BUT DO WE GET ANY THANKS FOR THAT? NO-O-O-O-O-O!"

John Trevor, *The Albuquerque Journal*. Reprinted with permission.

with respect to burglary and other property crimes, it is unlikely to have much effect on crimes of impulse, such as rape and many murders. They reason that people who are about to kill their wives in a rage are totally incapable of making any calculations at all. But this is far from obvious. The prisoners in Nazi concentration camps must frequently have been in a state of well-justified rage against some of their guards; yet this almost never led to their using violence against the guards, because punishment—which, if they were lucky, would be instant death, but was more likely to be death by torture—was so obvious and so certain. Even in highly emotional situations, we retain some ability to reason, albeit presumably not so well as normally.

It would take much greater provocation to lead a man to kill his wife if he knew that, as in England in the 1930's, committing murder meant a two-out-of-three chance of meeting the public executioner within about two months than if—as is currently true in South Africa—there were only a one-in-100 chance of being executed after about a year's delay. . . .

Fallacy of Rehabilitation

Finally, I should like to turn to the issue of why "rehabilitation" became the dominant rationale of our punishment system in the latter part of the 19th century and has remained so up to he present, in spite of the absence of any scientific support. The reasons, in my opinion, have to do with the fallacy, so common in the social sciences, that "all good things go together." If we have the choice between preventing crime by training the criminal to be good—i.e., rehabilitating him—or deterring crime by imposing unpleasantness on criminals, the former is the one we would like to choose.

The Reverend Sydney Smith, a follower of the deterrence theory, said a prison should be "a place of punishment, from which men recoil with horror—a place of real suffering painful to the memory, terrible to the imagination. . . a place of sorrow and wailing, which should be entered with horror and quitted with earnest resolution never to return to such misery. . . ." This is an exaggeration. Our prisons do not have to be that bad; the deprivation of liberty in itself may be a sufficiently effective punishment. But in any case, deterrence necessarily involves the deliberate infliction of harm.

Jails—The Ultimate Solution

The most important lesson research has taught is that there is only one thing government can surely do about criminals. It can lock them up—and then be secure in the knowledge that while in jail they are not out committing more crimes. And that's about all government can know. The notion that prison can rehabilitate was a dream that lived too long. It doesn't. Period.

Michael Kramer, *New York*, February 8, 1982.

If, on the other hand, we can think of the prison as a kind of educational institution that rehabilitates criminals, we do not have to consciously think of ourselves as injuring people. It is clearly more appealing to think of solving the criminal problem by means that are themselves not particularly unpleasant than to think of solving it by methods that are unpleasant. But in this case we do not have the choice between a pleasant and an unpleasant method of dealing with crime. We have an unpleasant method—deterrence—that works, and a pleasant method—rehabilitation—that (at least so far) never has worked. Under the circumstances, we have to opt either for the deterrence method or for a higher crime rate.

71

Distinguishing Between Fact and Opinion

When investigating controversial issues, it is important that one be able to distinguish between statements of fact and statements of opinion.

This activity is designed to help develop the basic reading and thinking skill of distinguishing between fact and opinion. Consider the following statement as an example: "Prisons are for incarcerating individuals who have committed punishable offenses." This statement is a fact with which virtually all would agree. But consider a statement which deals with the effect of prisons on the offender: "Prisons do not rehabilitate. Rather, they create and perpetuate a class of hard core offenders." Such a statement is clearly an expressed opinion. Rehabilitation programs vary from prison to prison, and the success of the programs vary. Not every prisoner is rehabilitated, but not every prisoner becomes a student in a prison's "school of crime."

Most of the following statements are taken from the viewpoints in this chapter. Consider each statement carefully. *Mark O for any statement you feel is an opinion or interpretation of fact. Mark F for any statement you believe is a fact.*

If you are doing this activity as a member of a class or group, compare your answers with those of other class or group members. Be able to defend your answers. You may discover that others will come to different conclusions than you. Listening to the reasons others present for their answers may give you valuable insights in distinguishing between fact and opinion.

If you are reading this book alone, ask others if they agree with your answers. You too will find this interaction very valuable.

O = opinion
F = fact

1. The cost of keeping one prisoner for one year is about $20,000—for far less than that the state could send the inmate to Smith College.

2. Work-release programs are probably the most constructive alternative to too much caging.

3. Young Americans are taught that trial by jury is a right, freely given, but that is not so.

4. There are more homicides per year in New York City than in France and Britain combined.

5. Deterrence theory holds that criminal behavior is influenced by the same types of cost/benefit incentives as any other type of economic activity.

6. As the costs or risks associated with a particular type of crime are increased, the attractiveness of that type of crime to potential offenders should decrease.

7. It is now universally recognized that a substantial number of inmates will not recidivate after their release, but there is little faith that the size of this fraction can be increased by rehabilitation programs.

8. Incarceration prevents those crimes that would have been committed by inmates during their period of incarceration.

9. Delinquent youths with strong self-discipline fare better in an unrestrictive setting than do those with weaker controls.

10. Those who believe that harsh penalties must again be exacted of criminals because treatment has failed are wrong.

11. Federal Bureau of Investigation statistics reveal that about one-third of released inmates are reincarcerated for a new offense.

12. A society may need a class of people against whom it is socially acceptable to vent aggression.

13. Changes in the age composition of the population seem to be closely tied to changes in the crime rate.

14. Prison should be a place of punishment, from which men recoil with horror—a place of real suffering painful to the memory.

15. Deterrence necessarily involves the deliberate infliction of harm.

Bibliography

The following list of periodical articles deals with the subject matter of this chapter.

Bennett H. Beach	"Getting Status and Getting Even," *Time*, February 7, 1983.
Mark W. Cannon	"Correcting Our Correction System: Alternative Sentencing and Prison Industry Programs," *Vital Speeches of the Day*, October 1, 1982.
Gay Cavender	"A Critique of Sanctioning Reform," *Justice Quarterly*, March 1984.
Nick Dispoldo	"Notes from a Prison Cell," *America*, May 8, 1982.
Lynne Goodstein, John Kramer, and Laura Nuss	"Defining Determinacy: Components of the Sentencing Process Ensuring Equity and Release Certainty," *Justice Quarterly*, March 1984.
Michael Kramer	"Keeping Bad Guys Off the Streets," *New York*, February 8, 1982.
Stephen Michaels and Hugh Aynesworth	"When One Murders," *Esquire*, March, 1983.
The New Guard	"Another Modest Proposal," Winter 1982-83.
Newsweek	"To Catch a Career Criminal," November 15, 1982.
Saturday Evening Post	"Making Criminals Pay Their Victims," January/February 1983.
Wilbert Rideau and Billy Sinclair	"Life: No Rhyme, No Reason," *The Angolite*, September-October 1982.
George F. Will	"The Value of Punishment," *Time*, May 24, 1982.
Lee Williams	"The Prison Rut," *Inquiry*, February 1983.
James Q. Wilson	"Dealing with the High-Rate Offender," *The Public Interests*, Summer 1983.
Universal Press Syndicate	"Prison Reform," *National Review*, May 14, 1982.

How Can Crime
Be Reduced?

"A more long-term response to crime is to attack its root causes."

Attacking the Roots of Violence Can Reduce Street Crime

David L. Bazelon

David L. Bazelon is Senior Circuit Judge for the US Court of Appeals for the District of Columbia and has sat on that bench since 1949. In addition, he is a lecturer on psychiatry at Johns Hopkins University School of Medicine and has received numerous awards for his work in the areas of psychiatry and the law from the American Psychiatric Association. In the following viewpoint, Judge Bazelon encourages the study of the underlying causes of violent crime. He states that the way to lessen terror on America's streets is to reform those responsible for the random wave of street crime.

As you read, consider the following questions:

1. According to the author, what is the most terrorizing type of crime?
2. What does the author think breeds crime?
3. Why does the author think that achieving social justice would achieve criminal justice?

David L. Bazelon, "Solving the Nightmare of Street Crime," reprinted from *USA Today*, January 1982. Copyright 1982 by Society for the Advancement of Education.

The nightmare of street crime is slowly paralyzing American society. Across the nation, terrified people have altered their lifestyles, purchasing guns and doubling locks to protect their families against the rampant violence outside their doors. After seething for years, public anxiety is now boiling over in a desperate search for answers. Our leaders are reacting to these public demands. In New York, Gov. Hugh Carey proposed the hiring of more police officers and prosecutors; in California, Attorney General Deuk Mejian has asked the legislature for immediate adoption of a package of new law enforcement bills.

A recent address by the Chief Justice of the United States has helped to place this crisis high on the public agenda. Speaking before the American Bar Association in February, Chief Justice Warren Burger described ours as an "impotent society," suffering a "reign of terror" in its streets and homes. The time has come, he declared, to commit vast social resources to the attack on crime—a priority comparable to the national defense.

Some have questioned whether a sitting Chief Justice should advocate sweeping changes in the criminal justice system and others have challenged his particular prescriptions, but I believe the prestige of his office has focused the nation's attention on issues critical to our future. We should welcome this opportunity to begin a thoughtful and constructive debate about our national nightmare.

In this debate, public concern is sure to generate facile sloganeering by politicians and professionals alike. It would be easy to convert this new urgency into a mandate for a "quick fix." The far-harder task is to marshall that energy toward examining the painful realities and agonizing choices we face. Criminologists can help make our choices the product of an informed, rational, and morally sensitive strategy. As citizens and as human beings, they have a special responsibility to contribute their skills, experience, and knowledge to keep the debate about crime as free of polemics and unexamined assumptions as possible.

I would like to outline some avenues of inquiry worthy of exploration. I offer no programs, no answers. After 31 years on the bench, I can say with confidence that we can never deal intelligently and humanely with crime until we face the realities behind it. First, we must carefully identify the problem that so terrorizes America. Second, we should seek to understand the conditions that breed those crimes of violence. Finally, we should take a close look at both the short- and long-term alternatives for dealing with the problem.

A reasoned analysis must begin by asking: What is it that has our society in such a state of fear? Politicians, journalists, and criminal justice professionals who should know better speak rather generally about "crime in America" without specifying exactly what they mean. There are, in fact, several distinct types of crimes and people who commit them.

Consider white-collar crime. This category embraces activities ranging from shoplifting to tax fraud to political corruption. It is undoubtedly a phenomenon of the gravest concern, costing society untold billions of dollars—far more than street crime. To the extent that such crimes appear to go unpunished, they breed disrespect for law and cynicism about our criminal justice institutions. Yet, as costly and corrosive as such crimes are, they do not instill the kind of fear reflected in the recent explosion of public concern. White-collar crimes, after all, are committed by the middle and upper classes, by "[p]eople who look like one's next-door neighbor," as sociologist Charles Silberman puts it. These people do not, by and large, threaten our physical safety or the sanctity of our homes.

Crime Linked to Childhood

Using in-depth behind-the-walls interviews of up to six hours' duration, researchers found further evidence linking parental violence during childhood with later adult criminal violence. And nearly 61 percent of the inmates' offenses were committed, according to inmate accounts, under the influence of alcohol, drugs or both.

Sam Newlund, *Minneapolis Tribune*, February 26, 1984.

Nor do the perpetrators of organized crime. After all, hired guns largely kill each other. The average citizen need not lock his doors in fear that he may be the object of gang warfare. Organized crime unquestionably does contribute to street crime—the most obvious connection is drugs—but organized crime has certainly not produced the recent hysteria.

Street Crime

Nor do crimes of passion cause us to bolt our doors so firmly at night. That would be like locking the fox *inside* the chicken coop. Clearly, it is the random assault of *street* crime—the muggings, rapes, purse snatchings, and knifings that plague city life—which puts us all in such mortal fear for our property and lives.

Once we focus on the kind of crime we fear, the second step in a constructive analysis is to identify those people who commit it. This is no pleasant task. The real roots of crime are associated with a constellation of suffering so hideous that, as a society, we can not bear to look it in the face. Yet, we can never hope to understand street crime unless we summon the courage to look at the ugly realities behind it. Nobody questions that street criminals typically come from the bottom of the socioeconomic ladder—from among the ignorant, the ill-educated, the unemployed, and the unemployable. A recent National Institute of Justice study confirms that our prison population is disproportionately black and young. The offenders that give city dwellers nightmares come from an underclass of brutal social and economic deprivation. Urban League president Vernon Jordan calls them America's "boat people without boats."

It is no great mystery why some of these people turn to crime. They are born into families struggling to survive, if they have families at all. They are raised in deteriorating, overcrowded housing. They lack adequate nutrition and health care. They are subjected to prejudice and educated in unresponsive schools. They are denied the sense of order, purpose, and self-esteem that makes law-abiding citizens. With nothing to preserve and nothing to lose, they turn to crime for economic survival, a sense of excitement and accomplishment, and an outlet for frustration, desperation, and rage.

Ghetto Youth

Listen to the words of a 15-year-old ghetto youth:

> In Brooklyn you fall into one of two categories when you start growing up. . . .First, there's the minority of the minority, the "ducks" or suckers. These are the kids who go to school every day. They even want to go to college. Imagine that! School after high school!
> . . .They're wasting their lives waiting for a dream that won't come true.
> The ducks are usually the ones getting beat up on by the majority group—the "hard rocks." If you're a real hard rock you have no worries, no cares. Getting high is as easy as breathing. You just rip off some duck. You don't bother going to school, it's not necessary. You just live with your mom until you get a job—that should be any time a job comes looking for you. Why should you bother to go looking for it? Even your parents can't find work.
> Hard rocks do what they want to do when they want to do it. When a hard rock goes to prison it builds up his reputation. He develops a bravado that's like a long sad joke. But it's all lies and excuses. It's a hustle to keep ahead of the fact that he's going nowhere. . . .

This, then, is the face behind the mask we call "the crime problem.". . .

Causes of Crime

A more long-term response to crime is to attack its root causes. This approach also offers no decisive balance of costs and benefits. The unique advantage of a successful attack on the roots of crime would be the promise of *enduring* social tranquility. If we can first break the cycle of suffering which breeds crime, we could turn it to our advantage. We would achieve more than "damage control." Our nation could begin to tap the resources of those we now fear. Instead of a police or garrison state, ours would then be a social order rooted in the will and hearts of our people. We would achieve criminal justice by pursuing social justice.

However, like the short-term solutions, this path would involve substantial risks and uncertainties. The root causes of crime are, of course, far more complex and insidious than simple poverty. After all, the vast majority of the poor commit no crime. Our existing knowledge suggests that the roots of street crime lie in poverty *plus*—plus prejudice, plus poor housing, plus inadequate education, plus insufficient food and medical care, and, perhaps most importantly, plus a bad family environment or no family at all.

Crime as a Type of Self-Employment

Most urban street crime is essentially self-employment that fills a small part of the vacuum created by the high levels of unemployment among young blacks and Hispanics. Compared with dead-end menial jobs and CETA jobs (both of which are now in short supply), robbery and drug peddling offer flexible hours, minimal risks, tax-free income and prestige among one's peers. In addition, the criminals can take advantage of welfare payments and food stamps and, while in prison, the free extension courses in crime skills offered by more experienced fellow inmates.

Bertram Gross, *The Nation*, February 6, 1982.

Accepting the full implications of what we know about street crime might require us to provide every family with the means to create the kind of home all human beings need. It might require us to afford the job opportunities that pose for some the only meaningful alternatives to violence. It would assure all children a constructive education, a decent place to live, and proper pre- and post-natal nutrition. It would seek to provide those children of inadequate family environments with proper day care or foster care. More fundamentally, it would seek to eradicate racism and prejudice.

Expensive Process

Such an attack on the roots of crime would obviously be an extremely long and expensive process. Before we can determine which programs offer the greatest promise, we must face what we know about the crime and build on previous efforts to attack its root causes.

More importantly, a genuine commitment to attacking the

roots of crime might force us to reconsider our entire social and economic structure. Like the short-term approach, this might conflict with other deeply held values. Can we break the cycle at crime's roots without invading the social sphere of the ghetto? Would this require the state to impose its values on the young? If we really want a lasting solution to crime, can we afford not to?

In short, any approach we take to crime presents attractive benefits and frightening risks. None of our choices offers a cheap or easy solution. Analysis takes us this far. As I have repeatedly emphasized, we can not choose which difficult path to take without facing the realities of street crime. Obviously, we can not deter those whom we do not understand. Nor can we make a rational assessment of incapacitation without knowing how many we will have to incapacitate and for how long. Finally, of course, we can not evaluate the long-term approach without some idea of its specific strategies and their various costs.

A constructive and fruitful debate about the best means of solving the nightmare of street crime is long overdue. The public's fear of crime cries out for a response and our leaders have made it a national priority, but we can never hope to achieve a just and lasting solution to crime without first facing the realities that underlie it. Emerson said, "God offers to every mind its choice between truth and repose." Truth will not come easy. It will take patience and the strength to put aside emotional reactions. If we do not strive for truth, this nation and all it stands for is bound to enjoy only a brief, false, and dangerous repose.

"It's up to citizens to take responsibility for themselves."

Community Involvement Can Reduce Street Crime

Frank Viviano

Frank Viviano is an associate editor at Pacific News Service (PNS) in San Francisco, California. Having a Ph.D. in social history from the University of Michigan, he joined the staff of PNS in 1979 and has since traveled and written extensively on politics and world immigration. In the following viewpoint, Mr. Viviano relates what he perceives as the dramatic success of a community crime watch program in Detroit.

As you read, consider the following questions:

1. What are some of the elements that helped reduce Detroit's crime problem?
2. How does Neighborhood Watch work?
3. Why do you suppose the police help set up Neighborhood Watch only on blocks where at least 50 percent of the residents actively participate?

Frank Viviano, "What's Happening in 'Murder City'," *The Progressive*, September 1981. Reprinted by permission from *The Progressive*, 409 Main Street, Madison, Wisconsin, 53703. Copyright © 1981, The Progressive, Inc.

These are not the best of times for the city of Detroit. At rush hour, the four expressways feeding workers into downtown are almost free of traffic. *The Detroit News,* which serves a metropolitan population of four million, carries just one and one-half columns of "help wanted" ads—many of them for jobs elsewhere. Hundreds of people line up outside drugstores for a look at the fat classified sections of newspapers imported from Houston and Los Angeles, the great magnets for the growing exodus of Michigan's unemployed.

LaVerne Jones of the Institute for Labor Research estimates that almost 350,000 workers in the Detroit area face permanent joblessness because of plummeting car sales and structural changes in the auto industry. . . .

Yet something unprecedented has happened in recent years which makes this far from the worst of times for Detroiters. With national paranoia over lawlessness soaring, Detroit seems to have beaten its own crime problem, which was once the nation's most acute. Its overall crime rate is down 30 per cent from three years ago. In one special target area, robbery has dropped by 56 per cent, breaking-and-entering by 61 per cent, rape by 60 per cent. . . .

The real story of Detroit's new peace is considerably more complicated than the solutions to crime undertaken in most places. It is the story of a city government that takes the concepts of community control and decentralization seriously. . . .

Constructing Detroit

Detroit was all of a piece in 1925, constructed so rapidly that its respective neighborhoods showed virtually no architectural variation, just as their respective inhabitants showed virtually no socioeconomic divergence. The job status and income of a Detroiter could be assessed simply by asking two questions: Where did she or he live, and in what style of house? It really was that simple, and for the most part, it remained that simple for thirty years.

Over those years, a mute, common understanding ruled Detroit—an understanding that certain residential barriers were not to be violated. Whatever the egalitarian rhetoric of the culture at large, Detroiters were born and raised in an atmosphere in which class consciousness was a palpable thing. Consequently, crime—omnipresent, terrifying street crime of the sort that characterizes American life today—remained under control, as it does in most societies where people know their place and where community feeling (for better or for worse) runs deep in every neighborhood.

But there was a fly in the ointment of strict class analysis in Detroit, the same fly that buzzes through every assessment of social and economic conflict in America. The fly was race, and in the years between 1950 and 1974 it made life in Detroit and unrelieved nightmare.

As the postwar consumer age produced ever greater demands on the auto industry, Detroit's working population grew apace, reaching a high of just under 1.9 million in 1950—still packed into those blocks which half a million fewer people had called home twenty-five years earlier. And the lot of the 400,000 of those cramped citizens who were black was by far the worst, as they were forced to remain in the tiny ghetto near downtown which had already been dubbed ''black bottom'' long before World War II labor needs had doubled and then tripled the black population. Suburban development could relieve the crowding in white neighborhoods, but for blacks the crowding created greater pressures with each passing year.

White Flight

It was, in short, an intolerable situation, which the subsequent history of Detroit revealed in brutal fashion, pitting working-class whites against working-class blacks in a neighborhood-by-neighborhood battle for living space. There were two discernible results: white flight, which reduced the white population from more than 1.5 million to 350,000 by 1978, and a phenomenal level of crime—not because the city had become black, but because its neighborhood stability had been shattered. In the years which saw Detroit descend into its ''Murder City'' period, it was a metropolis almost entirely given over to transience. The sense of community feeling is difficult to preserve in a forest of ''for sale'' signs.

Community Crime Prevention

The most promising direction in crime prevention, I think, is to go beyond protecting individuals from victimization into conceiving crime prevention activities as part of community development projects which strengthen informal social controls in the neighborhood.

Diana R. Gordon, *Vital Speeches of the Day*, February 11, 1983.

That brings us to the bottom of the abyss—the bloody 1967 riots that killed at least forty-three Detroiters and left much of the city a smoking ruin. For the Chandler Park area, which until that year was racially divided by the park of the same name, the riots opened a truly unpleasant half-decade. Black and white families alike were victimized by gangs operating out of the neighborhood's hundreds of abandoned houses, despite a massive investment in police manpower and tactical mobile units, which only seemed to exacerbate the problem. From 1970 to 1974, burglary, larceny, and auto theft increased by 61.6 per cent. "Everyone on our block—absolutely everyone—was robbed one year," remembers Alice Szawicz, one Chandler Park resident. "Even two policemen."

Nevertheless, the bottom had been reached, for the simple reason that Chandler Park, like the city that surrounded it, was no longer racially divided.

In effect, the riots broke down the barriers which had once kept Detroit's classes—and later its races—separate. In 1966, the city had three sorts of neighborhood: black, becoming black, and all-white. By 1978 there was not a single all-white neighborhood. The riots had accelerated white flight to the suburbs and blacks had moved into disintegrating white neighborhoods; later, white flight slowed, and the staggering difference between housing costs in the inner city and the suburbs began to draw some young whites into neighborhoods that had once been entirely black.

Detroit had entered 1967 as one of the most thoroughly segregated cities in the United States. When it finally emerged from the ashes of that year's riots a decade later, it was perhaps the most fully integrated of the nation's cities. Slowly, a consensus began to emerge out of the ashes as well. Race wasn't the problem any more; crime was. And in the eyes of many Detroiters, the police were demonstrably not the solution.

Alienated Community

Police Department spokesman Fred Williams, a twenty-five-year veteran of the force, quickly agrees that there was something wrong with the police—and with police policy—in those years. "Basically, we used to just tell people what was wrong, and how we're going to take care of it," he says. "But the more police had their way, the more they alienated the community. And in the meantime, the crime rate kept rising."

With the 1974 election of Coleman Young, the city's first black mayor, came the first important steps toward a different approach. Young had run on a specific promise to the black community: He would get rid of Detroit's STRESS squad, the "SWAT"-like decoy unit which many blacks regarded as a legalized death squad, licensed to kill teen-aged blacks involved in petty property crimes. Young kept his promise and improved on it, establishing an aggressive affirmative action program to recruit black officers into the predominantly white police force. The program soon began to pay off in improved trust between the department and the entire community.

"Detroit's like a big, big little town," says Fred Williams.

"Once the racial makeup of the police force reflected the reality of the population, nearly everybody had a friend or a relative in law enforcement. It wasn't 'them' any more; it was 'us.'" But that still wasn't enough.

Late in 1976, Young named William L. Hart police chief, with a mandate to study the problem of crime in Detroit and make whatever changes were necessary to meet it. Hart reached some drastic conclusions about his department: Even with the improved racial climate, nothing seemed to work. "Traditional police practices," he flatly states, "will not reduce crime." In fact, Hart told the mayor, the police themselves could do very little once crimes had actually been committed. If crime was to be reduced at all, "the citizens in the community must be actively involved."

Community Involvement

Community involvement, of course, is not a new phrase in the vocabulary of American crime-fighting. But what Hart had in mind wasn't a paper program that amounted to little more than a public relations pitch for better cooperation with the old police methods. He was out to create a new way. He was out, in effect, to throw away the old book on crime—and to let the people of Detroit's neighborhoods rewrite it.

A Change of Heart

We *must* choose to get involved—not physically—not foolishly—but by seeking the right solutions. We must choose to care about what happens around us and in the courtroom. We must choose to care about our neighbor's safety as much as our own. Again, to quote our President, "The war on crime will only be won when an attitude of mind and a change of heart takes place in America."

James B. Jacobsen, *Vital Speeches of the Day,* August 1, 1982.

"You could say that we decided to be revolutionaries," says Williams. "We became community organizers."

The process started with a decentralizing scheme that saw fifty police "mini-stations" open all over town, staffed not only with police but also with some 2,000 trained volunteers, residents of the neighborhood who acted as links between the police and the local population. More important, perhaps, Hart shifted the emphasis of departmental policies away from "reactive" or after-the-fact police action and toward actual prevention of crime. Commander James L. Humphrey, a specialist in prevention methods, was put in charge of a massive effort to implement the new policy. Then the real changes began.

Those changes are evident in the way police officers George Preston and Herbert Kaltz spend their workday in Chandler Park, where I joined them last spring. The old days would have found Preston, a former narcotics officer, and Kaltz, who worked the tactical mobile unit, patrolling these blocks in a squad car. Today Preston and Kaltz—one black, one white—operate from a quiet office in the basement of Emmanuel Lutheran Church, and they are most likely to be found in a backyard or living room somewhere in the neighborhood—not solving crimes but talking to people about their lives and needs.

Changing Times

In a neat brick bungalow on Philip Street, eight blocks from the church, retired tire-plant worker John Petross tells the officers about the time he opened his front door one evening five years ago and found a rifle pointed at his belly. Petross decided it was time to leave Detroit. "I just can't live with this," he remembers thinking. But the next day, Petross changed his mind. "My wife and I were driving down Philip when it hit me: We panic and give our homes away. That's exactly what's wrong. The thing to do was clean the neighborhood up, not leave it."

A few blocks to the south, Alice Szawicz, a beautician, says she once came home from work and discovered a burglar in her living room. Like Petross, she thought about leaving. But also like Petross, Szawicz is a fighter; she doesn't give up easily.

And that, says George Preston, is what makes the difference between urban devastation and renewal. "We can throw everything we know into beating the crime problem around here, but we can't do it alone, and we can't really lead the way. It's up to folks like Alice and John, the natural leaders on the block. Our job is to make it possible for them to take responsibility for their own situation."

Neighborhood Watch

For the city's 112 crime-prevention officers, that job has meant canvassing door to door on foot in search of neighborhood leaders to host block meetings. It has meant getting leaflets to every household, conducting 4,000 residential and business security surveys to advise on precautionary equipment—locks, bars, alarms—and speaking to 500,000 Detroiters in 7,000 different community meetings since 1976.

After the first meeting, which is primarily social, the officers begin a detailed discussion of prevention strategies ranging from ways to frustrate burglary to self-protection in the street. "Neighborhood Watch" and the larger program built around it are meant to serve as much more than inducements for neighbors to watch out for suspicious strangers. On each block, the program functions as a general clearinghouse for information relating to "safe urban living." At regular intervals, the police make free "security surveys" of individual homes, on appointment, and provide counsel on changes in locks, windows, or shrubbery. In the city's two target areas, senior citizens were given equipment necessary to effect such changes, and the equipment was installed by local merchants, neighbors, and the area's crime prevention unit policemen. . . .

Personal Safety

When the training ends, large signs bearing the name of the community organization are erected at each end of the block. The signs are "psychological barriers against crime," says Lieutenant Norbert Kozlowski, assistant director of the Crime Prevention Program. "They indicate that the block is organized, that these people are not easy victims."

But this is where the crucial catch applies. Neighborhood Watch only goes past the second meeting if 50 per cent of the block's residents actively participate. In the east-side target area where Preston and Kaltz work, some 100 blocks have failed to meet the 50 per cent involvement requirement. "We must have citizens who accept responsibility and get involved," insists Chief Hart.

So far, 3,500 Neighborhood Watch organizations have been incorporated in the city, and police have strong evidence in support of their effectiveness. In the first two and one-half years of the program in another special target area on the west side, crime fell overall by 65 per cent. And when a follow-up team looked into the area's burglary total for the last year, it discovered an even more remarkable fact: Every break-in involved a home that was not actively participating in Neighborhood Watch.

But for those which do participate, the benefits often far exceed improved security. "The idea is making a better place in as many ways as possible," says Preston. The by-products of community organization in Preston's district range from a neighborhood van service for senior citizens to a noticeable reduction of "for sale" signs on front lawns.

"Victim behavior during the event may have dramatic consequences for the outcome."

Victim Behavior Modification Can Reduce Crime

Ezzat A. Fattah

Ezzat A. Fattah is a professor in the Department of Criminology at Simon Frazer University, Burnaby, British Columbia. The following viewpoint is excerpted from an article he contributed to *Crime & Delinquency*, a journal for professionals in the field of criminal justice. In it, Mr. Fattah argues that more research on victim behavior before a crime is committed and after the act will help determine how citizens can prevent becoming victims.

As you read, consider the following questions:

1. According to a Braithwaite and Biles survey, who are particularly vulnerable to serious crime?
2. What does the author think is the victim's choice concerning whether or not to resist an attack?
3. How does Mr. Fattah think that victim's reactions during a crime affect their psychological response to the experience?

Ezzat A. Fattah, "Victims' Response to Confrontational Victimization: A Neglected Aspect of Victim Research," Vol. 30 No. 1, January 1984, pgs. 75-89. Copyright © 1984 by Sage Publications, Inc. Reprinted by permission of Sage Publications Inc.

For over a century, criminologists have been preoccupied with elucidating the causes of crime and developing a theory of criminal behavior. Criminology theories identify myriad biological, psychological, and social factors as causing or contributing to crime, but it seems strange that no comprehensive theory of victim's behavior has been developed. Such a theory would be invaluable for understanding the crime phenomenon and indispensable for developing an effective strategy for crime prevention. In many cases, the victim's behavior does play an important, perhaps a determining role, in the motivational phase and in the causal process leading to the commission of the crime. Often the denouement of the crime drama is a function of the victim's response to the criminal's initiative. Once the crime has been committed, the victim's decision to notify or not to notify the police determines whether or not the criminal justice system will be mobilized. Last but not least, the victim's behavior as a witness may have a great impact on the outcome of the judicial process and may be influential in whether or not the criminal will be punished.

It seems obvious, however, that greater attention should be paid to the victim. . . .

Research on Victimization

In recent years our knowledge of the nature, extent, and patterns of criminal victimization has been enhanced through research on the victims of specific crimes and by a wealth of information from victimization surveys conducted in many countries. We now know that crime victims are not chosen at random and that the risks of victimization are neither randomly nor equally distributed within the general population. For example, the chances that a black resident of New York will be a victim of criminal homicide are eight times higher than for a white resident of the same city. Criminological literature is full of data asserting differential rates of victimization. We know, therefore, that crime victims do not constitute an unbiased cross-section of the population. And we know that most criminals—and, above all, professional criminals—choose their victims carefully and make subtle distinctions between appropriate and inappropriate targets.

But what makes a person, a residence, a business, or a car an attractive or easy target? What personal or environmental characteristics render a person prone to criminal victimization? What type of behavior or lifestyle increases the level of risk exposure and consequently the hazards of victimization? The answers to all these questions remain, at best, tentative. One important and interesting finding of victimization surveys in the United States is that victimization rates are closely linked to the characteristics of victims—especially to age, sex, marital status, family income, and race (Hindelang et al., 1978: 4). Another important finding is that personal characteristics associated with risks of victimization are rather stable across cities. Hindelang, Gottfredson, and Garofalo (1978) found that in all of the cities where surveys had been done, younger persons had much greater rates of personal victimization than did older persons; similarly, males had higher rates than did females, and single persons had higher rates than married persons. They noted:

> Although *levels* of victimization showed considerable heterogeneity across cities the patterns of association between victimization and most demographic characteristics were strikingly similar regardless of the individual city examined. This was not only true for personal characteristics that are associated with risks of victimization but also for many characteristics of the incidents themselves—the extent of reporting to the police, the nature and extent of physical injury and financial loss, and so on—particularly when the focus is on the correlates of these characteristics [1978: 4].

On the basis of Australian survey data, Braithwaite and Biles (1979) found that the unemployed are particularly vulnerable to being victims of some of the more serious types of crime. They suffer a high rate of theft victimization and a staggeringly high rate of assault victimization.

Both American and Australian data strongly suggest that there is a strong positive correlation between the risk of being personally victimized and the proportion of time the person spends in public places.

Reprinted by permission. Tribune Media Services Inc.

Using victimization survey data, Hindelang et al. (1978) formulated a tentative theory of personal victimization. Lifestyle is a central component in their theoretical model. The centrality of lifestyle derives primarily from its close association with exposure to victimization risk situations. Because different lifestyles imply different probabilities that individuals will be in particular places at particular times under particular circumstances, and interacting with particular kinds of persons, lifestyle affects the probability of victimization. . . .

Victim's Response

Becoming a victim is not a matter of choice. Most victims do not voluntarily assume this role, but are forced into it through the offender's behavior. The victim's response to the unwanted and usually unexpected victimization is, to a large extent, unpremeditated and unplanned. The spontaneity of the reaction is no doubt responsible for the extreme variations in victims' response to identical situations and to very similar victimization experiences. The same offensive behavior, be it assault, rape, or robbery, does not elicit identical reactions from all those being victimized. . . .

Profile of a Victim

A rapist may select his victim by the way she walks down the street, according to the results of two recent research projects. One study suggests that rapists may look for women who appear to be submissive and lacking in confidence and determination, in the way muggers prey on pedestrians who appear oblivious, dazed or disoriented.

Jeff Meer, *Psychology Today*, May 1984.

Not all victims give in when they find themselves face to face with a burglar, a mugger, a hold-up man, an extortionist, a rapist, or a kidnapper. Some will attempt to defend themselves or to protect their property with quite exceptional vigor. Such behavior may trigger a violent attempt to subdue or to silence the victim on the part of an aggressor who is himself tense and fearful. . . .

Victim behavior during the event may have dramatic consequences for the outcome, and what the victim does during the actual victim-offender encounter often determines how the victimization experience will end. Researchers who have examined the victim's response have focused on two outcomes: the success or failure of the attack, and whether bodily harm has been caused to the victim. Future research may examine two additional dimensions: a time dimension and a psychological dimension. This would make it possible to distinguish four distinct outcomes: success or failure, duration of the ordeal, the physical outcome, and the psychological outcome.

Success or Failure?

Success or failure is usually operationalized in terms of completion or incompletion of the crime. For example, if the rape or robbery is completed, it is considered a success, and if the crime remained at the stage of attempt, it is counted as failure. The outcome may be more broadly defined as successful if the attacker was able to execute his plan and achieve his goal totally or partially. It may be designated a failure if the victimizer was forced to abandon his original plan or was unable to fulfill his goal. With sufficient empirical data, the probabilities of success or failure for each specific response could be established in relation to specific types of victimization. As of now, we can only say that active resistance is, in general terms, inversely related to robbery and rape completion.

Many Citizens Are Cowards

Criminals see that the average citizen is a coward. You might protest the use of the word coward, but how would you describe the following: thugs get on a crowded subway car. They jostle and harass a few passengers, robbing them in full view of other passengers. These spectators just crowd together and hope the thugs won't bother them. What they should do is make sure that the next light of day these thugs see is through the window of an intensive care unit—three days later.

Walter E. Williams, *The Union Leader*, September 24, 1981.

In general, the shorter the ordeal, the less suffering the victim goes through. The effectiveness of the victim's response may therefore be assessed not only in terms of its impact on the success or failure but also in relation to the duration of the ordeal. Certain responses are likely to prolong the duration of the victimization experience while other responses are likely to hasten its termination.

The amount of force employed against the victim, whether injury has been inflicted or not, and the nature and extent of injury depend in many cases on the victim's reaction. Certain types of response are more likely to elicit a violent reaction on the part of the offender than are others. These responses endanger the physical integrity of the victim and enhance the chances that he or she will be killed or physically injured. On the basis of available evidence there seems to be no doubt that resistance by the victim escalates the level of force employed by the offender. Hindelange et al. (1978) found that the victim's use of a physical force self-protective measure is the attribute most strongly associated with injury. The injury rate for those who used a physical self-protective measure (56%) was nearly three times greater than for victims who did not use such self-protective measures (20%). This is corroborated by Block's (1977) finding that robbery injury is determined by many factors—most important of which is victim resistance and the offender's weapon.

Every victimization does have a psychological impact and is likely to leave the victim with long-term or short-term emotional scars. Many victims suffer from psychological trauma, feelings of shame, embarrassment, guilt, humiliation, abandonment, and an enhanced sense of vulnerability. The psychological outcome depends, no doubt, on a large number of factors. And it is not unreasonable to assume that the way the victim responded to the attack would have an effect on the psychological outcome of the incident. Is it true, as some claim, that one of the positive effects of struggle is a reduction in the traumatic effects of victimization? Is it true that victims who actively resist may suffer more physical but less psychological injuries than those who consent, comply or submit? If we set aside arguments based merely on ideological positions, we can safely say that only research will tell.

"Without a job and without the hope of finding a job, the ex-inmate readily and understandably returns to crime."

Ex-Inmate Job Program Can Reduce Crime

Hilton L. Rivet

Hilton L. Rivet is New Orleans Archdiocese prison apostolate director and the former rector of the Jesuit community at Loyola University. A Roman Catholic priest and writer, he is the author of *Hey Lord, Can You Give Me a Minute?*, a book widely used by inmates to help them come to grips with their feelings. In the following viewpoint, Father Rivet claims that ex-inmates must have job training to resist the lure of crime.

As you read, consider the following questions:

1. Why does Father Rivet call his plan the *only* cure for crime?
2. According to the author, what occupation holds the most promise for ex-inmates?
3. How does the author expect the program to be self-supporting?

Hilton L. Rivet, "The Only Cure for Crime," *America*, February 7, 1981. Reprinted with permission of America Press, Inc. 106 West 56th Street, New York, NY, 10019. © 1981 All rights reserved.

Billions of tax dollars are being poured into the fight against crime. Yet the crime rate continues to increase not only in this country but throughout the world. Something is radically wrong. It would appear to be time to face reality and to look elsewhere for the solution rather than continue to pour more dollars into law enforcement, police equipment, correctional programs, new prisons and more and more new judicial seats. I would like to suggest a better way.

I call my plan, or dream, EXIN, Inc., because it refers to former prison inmates. It means that only exinmates from some prison somewhere can participate. The whole idea issues from the conviction that a man or woman who leaves prison more often than not carries a stigma with him or her. Society has rejected that person as an outcast, a reject, a loser. It refuses to give him or her a job, or at best give one at ridiculously low pay. Without a job and without the hope of finding a job, the exinmate readily and understandably returns to crime to supply his and his family's needs for survival in this very competitive society. This cycle must be interrupted; it can only be done by offering the exinmate a job. . . .

Dwell for a minute on the feelings that must prevail within the exinmate who returns to the outside world and finds himself completely rejected by the society that has already dehumanized and depersonalized him through the process of forcing him to serve time. The anger, hate and desire for revenge boiling within will inevitably spill out and act themselves out against society. Crime then becomes a way of life, a way forced upon the offender because there is no other avenue open to him. The recidivism rate remains high because the world has turned its back and refused to take the one necessary and indispensible step to help the offender to reclaim himself.

A person must reclaim his dignity in his own eyes. This can only be done by affording him hope for the future, hope based upon his own expectations that he will be able to do something worthwhile with his life. EXIN, Inc. would offer him an opportunity to become a part owner, a profit sharer, a respected businessman or woman in the marketplace. He will be a capitalist. He then can dream all the good dreams about his future: of a home, a wife and kids, a car, a boat, a trip around the world, nice clothes, meals at fancy restaurants, etc. In a word, he will be able to watch the television commercials and know that what they offer lies within his reach.

A Choice

The exinmate, moreover, can find meaning in those months, years or even decades, during which he served out his sentence. He would be asked in the early days of incarceration if he would like to participate in EXIN. He would be promised a job upon release. He is given, in other words, an opportunity to make a choice: whether he wants to turn his life around or continue in crime. There will always be those, of course, who prefer to make the quick buck through illegitimate and unlawful means. There will even be some who enjoy the game of cops and robbers. Without that excitement their lives would be too dull to endure. Certainly, there will be the "professional thieves" who refuse to give up their unique way of life. That, however, is their choice. No longer could they argue that there is no job available even if one wants to go straight. On the other hand, the ones who would profit from the offering will be legion.

The Incompatibility of Prison Life and Society

Men leaving prison today have little, if any, formal educaton; they do not have marketable skills; and they have poor work habits because prison has instilled that dependency complex in their characters. Many of today's ex-offenders cannot even read a job application form: they do not know how to dress for job interviews; and do not have the appropriate attitude to even land a job. Prison has not taught them any of these basic survival skills. Prison only teaches them that it's "count-time," "chow-time," or "no stopping on the Walk."

Wilbert Rideau and/or Billy Sinclair, *The Angolite*, November-December 1981.

Once having accepted the opportunity to become involved in EXIN, the person is then told that he must start immediately, while in prison serving his sentence, to prepare himself for the day of release and the claiming of his job. This, is effect, turns "dead time" into "live time," because day by day something is happening within that person that makes the day bearable because it is intimately related to his future life. Living takes on meaning, and when that happens a person is able to endure anything.

Training Programs

If EXIN is to be realistic, it must prepare men and women for businesses in which they can find a place; those for which training programs can begin while the inmates are still serving time in prison; those that allow for the expression of various levels of intellectual and vocational skills; those that are needed in the marketplace; those that will provide adequate remunerations in wages, fringe benefits and profit sharing for all engaged in them.

Of the many possible types of businesses that could be started, one especially measures up to the above criteria. It is fleet auto and truck maintenance and repair. There surely will always be automobiles and trucks that are in need of being maintained and repaired. This is the type of business that would provide jobs for both the totally illiterate, who might only be capable of sweeping floors and dusting car bodies, and the highly sophisticated, e.g., a person capable of bookkeeping for the corporation.

The inmate must be involved with the corporation while still in prison through study of automobile motors, generators, distributors, etc. If the prison is unwilling to provide a shop in which to work, then at least books with suitable diagrams can be studied and something worked out whereby bona fide mechanics can come in and do the instructing. In fact, in the state of Louisiana, where there is a great and growing emphasis on vocational schools, it would seem that the state should be more than willing to subsidize a large part of this operation in order to educate its citizenry, provide them with adequate jobs and emphatically reduce the crime rate.

Equal Employment

Both men and women could be equally employed in such a venture. There could be outlets all over the state, even several outlets in any one big city. In order to assure the maximum opportunity, it would be desirable to obtain contracts to service trucks for some large business enterprise (e.g., Coca-Cola, Brown's Velvet Ice Cream, 7-Up, etc.). A contract with any such company would be effected through the EXIN's business office and would render service to the trucks at a monthly rate with any replacement parts being paid for by the company that owns the trucks. As is obvious, this would involve a lot of paperwork which, of course, would provide more jobs for men and women coming out of prison and looking for work.

The EXIN program even suggests the possibility of other outlets for men and women coming out prison. One might call them supporting industries. Any man or woman, having profited from association with EXIN in their early days out of prison, should also feel free to leave EXIN and open their own businesses if they so wish. The plan obviously would also promote a spirit of work, rather than reliance upon the Government of welfare. It would genuinely bring forth the best in a man or a woman. It would give hope.

The governing board of EXIN, Inc. should be composed of both exinmates and of people who have never been incarcerated. This last, in all honesty, is intended to make sure not only that the operation stays "clean," but also that adequate expertise is available for the efficient functioning of the organization. These people should be intelligent, devoted and willing to give of their time and talents without any financial recompense.

Their reward will be that of seeing men and women functioning members of society. They will also be rewarded by seeing a reduction of crime in society.

EXIN, Inc. should begin immediately. There must, of course, first be a great deal of planning and thinking. A board needs to be formed. The ideas need to be discussed. Businessmen need to look at the pros and cons. Lawyers need to be involved. EXIN should be able to begin operating about a year after a board is organized and functioning.

Philanthropic Venture

An operation like this could use a quarter of a million dollars to get if off the ground. It would seem that philanthropic persons would risk very little in lending a large amount of money with the virtual assurance that it would be repaid over a long period of time. EXIN needs to be underwritten by foundations, Government programs, business trusts and the like. But in the long run, the money spent (and perhaps even lost in the beginning) would be nothing compared to the social and communal benefits that eventually would accrue to both EXIN members and the community in which they live.

There is admittedly the element of risk involved. EXIN is a daring proposal. But all great enterprises have started only because somebody has dared. It should be easy, moreover, to convince others that EXIN is timely, because for so long so much has been tried with little or no success that the community should be anxious to attempt something with men and women who are willing to try to save themselves instead of leaving it to the state to do it for them.

The state, in the long run, would save money by not having to house men and women in prisons at a cost of $20,000 per year, per person. It would gain because that many more people, former prison inmates, would begin paying taxes back to the state instead of subsisting on welfare. EXIN should have started yesterday. We should delay no longer.

"Criminal court judges could do much to relieve the situation by applying firmness and common sense to their criminal dockets."

A Firmer Court System Can Reduce Crime

James J. Kilpatrick

James J. Kilpatrick, one of the nation's most articulate and influential conservative journalists, is a regular columnist for *Nation's Business* and contributing editor to *National Review*. A former newspaperman, he is the author of *The Smut Peddlers, The Southern Case for School Segregation,* and *The Sovereign States: Notes of a Citizen of Virginia.* In the following viewpoint, Mr. Kilpatrick argues that lenient judges are to blame for allowing dangerous criminals to be set free.

As you read, consider the following questions:

1. What changes in the legal system does the author recommend?
2. What does he think is *most* essential to achieving a reduction in crime?
3. Why does the author think that "bail crime" can be eliminated?

James J. Kilpatrick, "Arresting Violent Crime," Reprinted by permission from NATION'S BUSINESS, July 1981. Copyright 1981, Chamber of Commerce of the United States.

A thick report came in the other day from the Federal Trade Commission having to do with public indifference to the hazards of smoking. The trouble with the present warning on a pack of cigarettes, said the staff, is that people have seen the notice so often they no longer really see it. The same anesthetic reaction, if I'm not mistaken, is developing in the matter of violent crime. We have grown numb to the appalling problem.

In a speech to the American Bar Association, Chief Justice Warren Earl Burger put the situation in blunt terms:

"Crime and the fear of crime have permeated the fabric of American life, damaging the poor and minorities even more than the affluent. . . .Today we are approaching the status of an impotent society whose capability of maintaining elementary security on the streets, in schools and for the homes of our people is in doubt."

No nation has a crime problem that approaches ours. The city of Washington last year had more criminal homicides than Sweden and Denmark combined. The United States has 100 times the burglary rate of Japan. We average one murder every 24 minutes, one forcible rape every 7 minutes, one violent crime every 27 seconds.

A Part of Life

The figures no longer impress. We have heard them too many times. Crime has become like the weather: Everybody talks about it, but there is a dispirited acceptance that nothing can be done about it. Crime is a part of life. No remedial measures can affect it.

Such defeatism is unworthy of a great and powerful country. We do not have to resign ourselves to a garrisoned society. There are steps that can be taken—practical, specific steps—that will help. Granted, little can be done about crimes of passion or quarrel-some assaults, but these are not the crimes that create the atmosphere of fear. We can begin by recognizing the enemy. He is the willful, deliberate criminal, to whom crime is in fact a way of life. If he can be caught and convicted and punished by a significant period of incarceration, some of the dreadful atmosphere may be dispelled.

Our criminal court judges could do much to relieve the situation by applying firmness and common sense to their criminal dockets. It is all well and good to have compassion for juveniles, but today's juvenile criminals are a different breed of young punks and hoodlums. The 17-year-old gunman is still a gunman. The 15-year-old mugger is still a mugger. They should be tried as adults and, if found guilty, punished as adults.

In his address the Chief Justice spoke of "the startling amount of crime committed by persons on release awaiting trial, on

JUSTICE UNDONE

PAROLE

SYSTEM

REPEATER CRIMINAL

SOCIETY

Don Hesse, *St. Louis Globe Democrat*. Reprinted with permission.

parole and on probation release.'' This is ''bail crime,'' and it can be greatly reduced if a determined effort is made to do so. It is absurd—dangerously, shamefully absurd—for defendants to be set free on bail when there is every commonsense reason to believe that they will commit new crimes before they can be tried for old ones.

Most jurisdictions now have laws that provide additional sentences for the use of a firearm in the commission of a felony.

With enough public pressure, judges can be impelled to impose these authorized punishments. Or given enough public pressure, we can get different judges who will impose them.

Appellate judges are in part responsible for the maddening delays and blatant miscarriages of justice that too often occur. Chief Justice Burger spoke of the need for "swift arrest, prompt trial, certain penalty and, at some point, finality of judgment." The interminable, frivolous, insubstantial appeals taken by jailhouse lawyers deserve swift and summary action.

The Answer: Improve the System

There is no reason to turn away in desperation as street crime increases to intolerable levels. The system that society has created for protection and security is the criminal justice system. If problems occur in that system, the answer is not to barricade ourselves in our homes, purchase handguns for portection, or form vigilante groups—the answer is to improve the system. As Supreme Court Justice Benjamin Cardozo stated, "The law, like the traveler, must be ready for the morrow. It must have the principle of growth."

James R. Thompson, *USA Today*, January 1982.

Without doing violence to Fourth Amendment rights, appellate judges could keep their eyes on the main question: Is the defendant guilty? The "exclusionary rule," which renders relevant and material evidence inadmissible, ought to be applied only in cases of grave abuse of civil rights by law enforcement officers.

Need for Changed Attitudes

The chief justice spoke of the need to provide our police and our prison guards with better training. Society can afford it. He asked for a sufficient number of investigators, prosecutors, public defenders and judges to bring defendants swiftly to trial. Society can afford it. He urged compulsory programs within our prisons to improve levels of inmate literacy and to provide job training. Such efforts may be futile in most cases—the record of rehabilitation is a melancholy record—but we must keep trying, and we can afford it.

What is needed above all, in my view, is a change in public attitudes. If we believe that present levels of violent crime are intolerable, let us tolerate these levels no longer. An apathetic people can accomplish nothing; an aroused people in time can win this war.

"Greater criminality has been associated with the rise of the welfare state and socialism."

Disbanding Social Programs Will Reduce Crime

Morgan O. Reynolds

Morgan O. Reynolds is associate professor of economics at Texas A & M University. He is the author of *Public Expenditures, Taxes, and the Distribution of Income: The United States, 1950, 1961, 1970.* The following viewpoint is based on his most recent work, *Crime by Choice.* In it, Mr. Reynolds claims that social programs are to blame for unemployment, demoralization, and the resulting high crime rate in the US.

As you read, consider the following questions:

1. Why does the author want to eliminate parole?
2. How does the author correlate the welfare state and crime rates?
3. According to the author, what is the role that private enterprise must play in the reduction of crime?

Morgan O. Reynolds, "How to Reduce Crime," *The Freeman*, March 1984. Reprinted by permission of the author.

Crime remains a silent contender for the number 1 domestic ill. It won't go away. Criminal experts are prone to explain this by saying that crime is "intractable," that there is little we can do. This claim is false. Crime is complex, to be sure, because it involves factors beyond law enforcement such as the strength of the family, neighborhoods, schools, and churches. But crime is simple in the sense that government officials can reduce crime by doing their job, namely, by making crime too unprofitable to practice.

No added resources are needed by the criminal justice system in order to accomplish this. Government finds it easy enough to spend money, but difficult to spend it productively. Between 1960 and 1982, for example, the number of serious crimes known to the police jumped from 3.3 million to 12.8 million, while government spending on police, courts, and corrections was doubling as a share of GNP, rising to one per cent of total output. Furthermore, victimization surveys show that only about one-third of crimes are reported to the police.

Thicket of Criminal Rights

The key to making our cities less dangerous is to change the rules of the game. We must reduce the enormous daily waste of time and effort that makes it so expensive to arrest, convict, and punish the guilty. While the machinery of government and its bureaucrats is always plagued by weak accountability and inefficiency, the law enforcement problem has increased dramatically over the last twenty years. Since 1961 the criminal justice system has been transformed from a law enforcement system into a thicket of criminal rights and make-work projects for nearly 2 million lawyers, judges, social workers, psychologists, criminologists, prison officials, and other bureaucrats. More people now produce less justice.

The quadrupling of crime over the past twenty years is due to a top-down revolution, as all revolutions in public policy are. Friedrich von Hayek points out that political opinion over the long run is determined by the active intellectuals. That is why in every country that has moved toward socialism, there was a long preceding phase during which socialist ideas governed the thinking of most intellectuals. Expanded rights for criminal defendants, sociological theories of crime, theories of rehabilitation, and dubious legal processes have followed the same path. . . .

The likely prospect is that things will get worse before they get better because criminal policies are still dominated by unsound ideas and unsound advisers. Legislatures are losing their earlier resolve and bowing to public pressure over the last few years. The people selling therapy for criminals are succeeding once again based on the argument that prisons are crowded and there is no sense in spending more money on failed policies. The legislature in Texas recently accepted this idea, pulling up short just as more plentiful and longer prison terms were beginning to make a dent in crime rates. So the first order of business is to fend off more of the same policies which caused the crime epidemic in the first place. . . .

Biased Criminal Procedures

In addition to discontinuing some things, the public sector should do some things that presently are not being done. The most important step is to rebalance our biased criminal procedures. It is no exaggeration to say that the Warren Court has the blood of thousands of crime victims on its hands. Without the ability to convict the guilty promptly and *conclusively* in fair if less-than-ideal procedures, nothing can substantially reduce crime. With all of the privileges granted to the accused in today's courts, we are fortunate to have as little crime as we have.

Massive Government Spending

Many of the social thinkers of the 1950s and '60s who discussed crime only in the context of disadvantaged childhoods and poverty-stricken neighborhoods were the same people who thought that massive government spending could wipe away our social ills. The underlying premise in both cases was a belief that there was nothing permanent or absolute about any man's nature—that. . .with government as the chief vehicle of change—we could permanently change man.

Ronald Reagan, address, September 28, 1981.

The techniques of the marketplace can improve the productivity of the public sector. Police departments, for example, should be at least partially rewarded on the basis of *gains* in reducing crime rates. The crime data should be checked by independent auditors. Private security agencies should be allowed to bid for contracts to supply police services where it is legally feasible. Based on experience, these measures can emerge on a piecemeal basis around the country, learning as we go. Similarly, private incentives and contractors can be more widely used in prosecution and corrections. When the duty of protecting a citizen from criminal harm is left solely to government, there are times due to neglect, malice, or political intrigue that prosecutors fail to act on behalf of the victim. If criminal law were amended to allow wider private rights of enforcement in the courts, then the citizen can protect himself if the government does not, and enforcement will be much more energetic. Prisoners should have more productive opportunities, with the profit motive allowed wider scope on both the demand and supply sides of the highly restricted market for prison labor services and in prison-made products. The ingenuity of the marketplace and competition should be harnessed to serve the cause of crime reduction. . . .

Eliminate Parole

We should eliminate false advertising: make sentences shorter but served in full. Sentences should fit the crime, not the criminal. The present philosophy about the appropriate procedures for determination of guilt and assignment of punishment basically should be reversed. Evidence about the accused's criminal background, for example, should be allowed in weighing the probability of guilt or innocence, but should be ignored for sentencing. We do it for traffic fines or tax evasion and should do it for criminal offenses as well. Perhaps juveniles should receive special consideration but punishment basically should fit the act, not the age nor the criminal record of the guilty party. One of the tragedies of the current arrangement is that juveniles initially receive tender-loving-care at the hands of the criminal system and are almost seduced into a criminal life. Not taking the system seriously, some of them end up serving long sentences as habitual criminals for crimes so old that nobody can remember them.

Severity of punishment can be humanely increased through greater use of solitary confinement. This serves the cause of justice because anti-social individuals and criminal bands destroy social cooperation, so let them bear the logical results of their actions. The English penal system used this technique with great success in days gone by, and their abandonment of the procedure has been a factor in the British crime epidemic. Solitary confinement also has the virtue of decreasing schooling in criminal skills and criminal contacts. Prisoners also should work, but I favor the carrot of productive, remunerative employment opportunities rather than the stick of breaking rocks all day. . . .

The Long Run

The rise of crime has not been an isolated social phenomenon. For instance, there is a striking parallel with the demise of discipline in the schools. Why? The basic reason is that a large, influential segment of public opinion came to believe that students should not be punished—made unhappy, reprimanded, scorned—for doing things that are wrong. As a substitute we ended up with "special counseling programs" and other non-answers. Those opposed to punishment share Rousseau's view of man, feeling that social constraints inhibit healthy human development, that people are born friendly and considerate. Propunishers believe that man is a mixture of good and bad, but that our basic instinct is to look out for number one and trample anyone who gets in the way of what we want. Under the weight of painful experience, our schools may be shifting away from Rousseau's views, but it can only be effective if adults are willing to face up to things, to show some backbone. Without serious steps to restrain the law-breaking minority, of course, the reversion to savagery is never far away.

Fortifying Social Foundations

Institutions that encourage positive norms and a sense of personal responsibility should be strengthened. If Americans successfully fortify the foundations of pro-social behavior, rather than simply combat the symptoms of anti-social behavior, some embryonic crime will be eliminated. We must focus on the roots of the problem—some of which are the beliefs, values, and attitudes being adopted by the young.

Mark W. Cannon, *Vital Speeches of the Day*, August 15, 1981.

The breakdown of the personal qualities of self-restraint, honesty, integrity, foresight, self-reliance, and consideration for others is indissolubly linked with the welfare state. For what is the redistributive state but a glorification of envy? There is an irreconcilable conflict between the rule of law, which depends on limited government, and the welfare state, which depends on a limitless government. As government has passed more and more laws and regulations, individual liberty has shrunk and disorder has grown. The rule of man has been substituted for the rule of law.

Crime and the Welfare State

The welfare state does not respect private property. It takes from the politically uninfluential and gives to the politically influential. Redistribution by government is not called stealing, though the same act is if performed by a private individual rather than a government official. Neither shoplifters nor more serious criminals think of themselves as stealing; they say that they just "take" things. In a way, they are right because crime and most of what takes place under the heading of politics amount to the same thing.

Changing the incentives faced by criminals is relatively easy from a technical point of view. Just make punishment swift, sure, and severe. It requires a firm but limited government. But if government is to restore the rule of law and protect private property, government itself must abide by the law. And this is not consistent with the welfare state.

Collectivists like to say that a war on poverty is also a war on crime. I agree with this statement but not in the sense that collectivists mean it. Collectivists mean more coerced redistribution, generous welfare benefits, more social workers and bureaucrats. The consequences of these programs have been family dissolution, illegitimacy, mass unemployment, demoralization, and non-existent work skills. Redistribution perpetuates poverty, intensifies it, and therefore increases crime. The real war on poverty occurs daily in the marketplace. Capitalism, entrepreneurship, commerce, and the creation of new wealth is the real war on poverty. Capitalism encourages independence, self-reliance, honest dealing, expanded employment opportunities, and therefore less crime.

Private Jobs

New job opportunities in the private sector reduce the relative attractiveness of crime and do not call for more government training and welfare programs. They demand less welfarism. Government should get out of the way and allow the marketplace to create more opportunities and wealth. Many factors influence the labor market conditions that potential criminals confront. For example, federal minimum wage laws and union wage rates prevent many young people, whose services are not worth $3.35 or more per hour, from finding legitimate work. Stealing then is more attractive because they cannot find occasional jobs to pick up spending money. They also fail to acquire the skills, like basic reliability, that would allow them to raise their value in the marketplace. Many other policies adversely affect crime rates, including monetary and fiscal policies. The graduated tax rates, for example, used to finance destructive social programs retard economic growth and employment opportunities.

Robbery and tyranny by the state is a reflection of the general breakdown of moral law, as it was in ancient Rome, when people had lost all respect for the sanctity of private property. If the lights go out in any major American city, many thousands of people will go on a crime spree, as they did in New York City in the blackout of 1977. The intellectuals have spent decades telling people that they are underdogs in an unjust and decaying society, and that violating the laws against theft or rape is a form of social protest, a form of higher morality.

The long run problem of producing more considerate people means greater reliance on the private market and less on government. It is no surprise that a decline in criminal behavior occurred with the growth of capitalism, and that greater criminality has been associated with the rise of the welfare state and socialism. Reviving internal constraints means gradually reversing the growth of Leviathan. If we are to solve the problem of crime, as with other ills of the welfare state, we must work toward a society where economic and social policies are determined by free markets, not centralized coercion.

The underlying problem is to change the intellectual climate in this country toward liberty and justice and away from collectivism and injustice. No one can avoid this intellectual battle in our politicized era. The purpose of the criminal justice system must become the pursuit of justice once again.

Distinguishing Bias from Reason

The subject of crime and criminals often generates great emotional responses in people. When dealing with such a highly controversial subject, many will allow their feelings to dominate their powers of reason. Thus, one of the most important basic thinking skills is the ability to distinguish between opinions based upon emotion or bias and conclusions based upon a rational consideration of the facts.

Most of the following statements are taken from the viewpoints in this chapter. The rest are taken from other sources. Consider each statement carefully. *Mark R for any statement you believe is based on reason or a rational consideration of the facts. Mark B for any statement you believe is based on bias, prejudice or emotion. Mark I for any statement you think is impossible to judge.*

If you are doing this activity as the member of a class or group compare your answers with those of other class or group members. Be able to defend your answers. You may discover that others will come to different conclusions than you. Listening to the rationale others present for their answers may give you valuable insights in distinguishing between bias and reason.

If you are reading this book alone, ask others if they agree with your answers. You too will find this interaction very valuable.

R = a statement based upon reason
B = a statement based on bias
I = a statement impossible to judge

1. The time has come to commit vast social resources to the attack on crime—a priority comparable to the national defense.

2. It is the random assault of street crime which puts us all in such mortal fear for our property and lives.

3. A recent National Institute of Justice study confirms that our prison population is disproportionately black and young.

4. The staggering difference between housing costs in the inner city and the suburbs began to draw some young whites into neighborhoods that had once been entirely black.

5. It's up to citizens to take responsibility for themselves, and up to police to help them do it wisely and safely.

6. The victim's behavior as a witness may have a great impact on the outcome of the judicial process.

7. It seems obvious that greater attention should be paid to the victim.

8. On the basis of available evidence there seems to be no doubt that resistance by the victim escalates the level of force employed by the offender.

9. Without a job and without the hope of finding a job, the ex-inmate readily and understandably returns to crime.

10. No nation has a crime problem that approaches ours.

11. It is all well and good to have compassion for juveniles, but today's juvenile criminals are a different breed of young punks and hoodlums.

12. The interminable, frivolous, insubstantial appeals taken by jailhouse lawyers deserve swift and summary action.

13. Prisoners also should work, but I favor the carrot of productive, remunerative employment opportunities rather than the stick of breaking rocks all day.

14. The breakdown of the personal qualities of self-restraint, honesty, integrity, foresight, self-reliance, and consideration for others is indissolubly linked with the welfare state.

15. If government is to restore the rule of law and protect private property, government itself must abide by the law.

Bibliography

The following list of periodical articles deals with the subject matter of this chapter.

Richard Allinson and Joan Potter	"Is New York's Tough Juvenile Law a *'Charade'?'' Corrections Magazine*, April 1983.
Doug Bandow	"Throw Lawyers at Them," *Conservative Digest,* January 1983.
Jerry Bergman	"The Influence of the Religious Belief in an Afterlife on Homicide," *The American Atheist,* January 1984.
William K. Coblentz	"A Glut of Lawyers," *Newsweek,* June 27, 1983.
Timothy Foote	"American Scene in New York: Be Kind to Your Mugger," *Time,* February 21, 1983.
Dave Jackson	"Victims of Crime Turn the Other Cheek," *Christianity,* April 9, 1982.
James B. Jacobson	"Victim Advocate: A New Style of Crime Fighter," *Ms.,* September 1982.
Patsy Klaus and Carol B. Kalish	"The Severity of Crime," *Bureau of Justice Bulletin,* January 1984.
A. Pivowitz and M. H. J. Farrell	"Now: Benefits for Crime Victims—A State by State Report," *Good Housekeeping,* January 1983.
Jon Garth Murray	"Justice and the Trickle-Down Theory," *The American Atheist,* March 1983.
Richard Neely	"The Politics of Crime," *Atlantic Monthly,* August 1982.
Society	Special section on Crime, July/August 1982.
Bertel M. Sparks	"A Legal System for a Free Society," *The Freeman,* March 1983.
Michael Spector	"Communist Corrections: The Untried Alternative to Prisons," *The Nation,* March 13, 1982.
Jay Stuller	"Runaway Law: Our Litigous Society," *The American Legion,* July 1983.

How Should White Collar Crime Be Controlled?

"Capital punishment for the corporation is one possibility."

Stricter Penalties Would Reduce Corporate Crime

John Braithwaite and Gilbert Geis

John Braithwaite is a research criminologist at the Australian Institute, Canberra, Australia. He is the author of *Reaffirming Rehabilitation* and numerous publications on the various aspects of corporate crime and criminal justice. Gilbert Geis is a professor of social ecology at the University of California at Irvine. He has taught at the Harvard Law School, the University of Oklahoma, and California State University and is the author of *Juvenile Gangs* and *Not the Law's Business?*. In the following viewpoint, the authors suggest that a new set of laws be legislated to deter corporate crime.

As you read, consider the following questions:

1. Why do the authors think that incapacitation as punishment should be revived?
2. According to the authors, what would be an effective deterrent to corporate crime?
3. How do the authors think that convicted corporations can be punished without hurting the economy or employees?

John Braithwaite and Gilbert Geis, "On Theory and Action for Corporate Crime Control," April 1982, *Crime and Delinquency.* © 1982 by the National Council on Crime and Delinquency. Reprinted by permission of Sage Publications Inc.

Traditional criminals can be incapacitated if the society is willing to countenance severe solutions. If we execute murderers, they will never murder again; or we can lock them up and never let them out. Pickpockets can be incapacitated by our cutting off their hands. Most contemporary societies are not prepared to resort to such barbaric methods. Instead, the widely used punishment is imprisonment for periods of months or years. Yet only partial incapacitation is in effect while the offender is incarcerated. Offenders continue to murder, to rape, and to commit a multitude of less serious offenses while they are in prison. Indeed, the chances of being a victim of homicide in the United States are five times as high for white males inside prison as for those outside. And the partial incapacitation of prison lasts only as long as the sentence.

The limits of incapacitation as a policy become more apparent when we ask who is to be incapacitated. A substantial body of evidence shows that no matter how we attempt to predict dangerousness, the success rate is very low. Any policy of selective incarceration to "protect society" will result in prisons full of "false positives.". . .

Preventing More Crime

Incapacitation is more workable with corporate criminals because the kind of criminal activity is dependent on their being able to maintain legitimacy in formalized roles in the economy. We do not have to cut off the hands of surgeons who increase their income by having patients undergo unnecessary surgery. All we need do is deregister them. Similarly, we can prevent people from acting in such formal roles as company directors product safety managers, environmental engineers, lawyers, and accountants swiftly and without barbarism. Should we want only short-term incapacitation, we can, as Stone advocates, prohibit a person "for a period of three years from serving as officer, director, or consultant of a corporation. . . ." Moreover, an incapacitative court order could be even more finely tuned. The prohibition could be against the person's serving in any position entailing decision making that might influence the quality of the environment. Corporate crime's total dependence on incumbency roles in the economy renders possible this tailor-made incapacitation. It makes the shotgun approach to incapacitation for common crimes look very crude indeed. However, the substitution problems that plague traditional incapacitative models are also a major constraint on the efficacy of incapacitating individuals who have been responsible for corporate crime. If, for example, the corporation is committed to cutting corners on environmental emissions, it can replace one irresponsible environmental engineer with another who is equally willing to

116

violate the law.

This is where court orders to incapacitate the whole organization become necessary. Capital punishment for the corporation is one possibility. The charter of a corporation can be revoked, the corporation can be put in the hands of a receiver, or it can be nationalized. Although corporate capital punishment is not as barbaric as execution of individual persons, it is an extreme measure which courts undoubtedly would be loath to adopt, especially considering the unemployment caused by terminating an enterprise (although this does not apply to nationalizing it). Even though court-ordered corporate death sentences may be politically unrealistic, there are cases where regulatory agencies through their harassment of criminal corporations have bankrupted fairly large concerns.

Limiting Company Charters

A less draconian remedy is to limit the charter of a company by preventing it from continuing those aspects of its operations where it has flagrantly failed to respect the law. Alternatively, as

Angelo Franco, *The Columbus Ledger-Enquirer*. Reprinted with permission.

part of a consent decree, a corporation could be forced to sell that part of its business which has been the locus of continued law violation. The participation of the regulatory agency in the negotiations would serve to ensure that the sale was to a new parent with an exemplary record of compliance. This kind of remedy becomes increasingly useful in an era when the diversified conglomerate is the modal form of industrial organization. Forcing a conglomerate to sell one of its divisions would, in addition to having incapacitative effects be a strong deterrent in cases where the division made sound profits. Deterrence and incapacitation can be achieved without harm to the economy or to innocent employees.

Effective incapacitative strategies for corporate crime are, therefore, possible. All that is required is for legislatures, courts, and regulatory agencies to apply them creatively to overcome the conservatism that leaves them clinging to the failed remedies carried over from traditional crime. The goal of incapacitation illustrates better than any other how the effective and just means for achieving criminal justice goals cannot be the same with corporate crimes as with traditional crime. Consider, for example, the application to the Olin Mathieson Chemical Corporation of a law that forbids offenders convicted of a felony from carrying guns. [Author Morton] Mintz has described what happened after Olin Mathieson was convicted of conspiracy concerning bribes to get foreign aid contracts in Cambodia and Vietnam:

> It happened that there was a law which said in essence that a person who had been convicted of a felony could not transport a weapon in interstate commerce. This created a legal problem for Olin, because it had been convicted of a felony, was in the eyes of the law a person and had a division that made weapons for use by armed forces. Congress resolved the dilemma by enacting a law that, in effect, got Olin off the hook.

A Fundamental Impediment

Here we are struck by the absurdity of automatically applying to corporations an incapacitative policy designed for individuals. It will be argued later that this absurdity of applying law governing the behavior of individuals to the crimes of collectivities is the fundamental impediment to effective corporate crime control. . . .

It has been argued that the largely discredited doctrines of crime control by public disgrace, deterrence, incapacitation, and rehabilitation could become highly successful when applied to corporate crime. More generally, it has been argued that when the accumulated insight of criminology tells us that something is true of traditional crime, in many respects we can expect the opposite to be true of corporate crime.

Hence, there is reason for optimism that where we have failed with street crime, we might succeed with suite crime. There is justification for regarding President Reagan's signaling of a return to pre-Watergate criminal justice priorities as contrary to the public interest. Because corporate crime is more preventable than other types of crime, the persons and property of citizens can be better protected; and restitution is a more viable goal for corporate than for traditional criminal law. Convicted corporations generally have a better capacity than do individuals to compensate the victims of their crimes.

Even though corporate crime is potentially more preventable and its victims are more readily compensated, there is no guarantee that either prevention or restitution will happen under traditional legal systems. This is because of our third proposition: Convictions are extremely difficult in complex cases involving powerful corporations. There are at least two ways of dealing with this problem. One is for regulatory agencies to achieve the goals of deterrence, incapacitation, and rehabilitation by non-prosecutorial means. They readily can do this if they have sufficient bargaining power. . . .

When a Worker Is Killed

When a worker has been injured or killed because of the violation of a safety law, the company may have to pay compensation, but such costs are generally not high enough to motivate the company to prevent other similar injuries or deaths. The employee's family may well be in a critical financial position, and in such a case simply countering a claim can result in a lower settlement. As a lawyer involved in a silicosis compensation case said, "With a maximum liability of only $12,500 plus medical and funeral expenses, it has been so inexpensive to disable and kill a man. . . that it has not been worthwhile to clean up."

Frank Henry, *Criminal and Social Justice*, Winter 1982.

Corporations will fight vigorously attempts to deny them any due process protections that are available to individuals. Yet the law of individualism can never be effective against the crimes of collectivities. As Fisse has observed, "[I]ndividualistic strength is not enough to match collectivist might without undermining the very traditions of justice for which individualism stands." Unless we can accept corporate crime as a conceptually separate problem from traditional crime, the powerful will continue to ensure that "collectivist might" prevails in courts of law. This will be achieved by appeal to "the very traditions of justice for which individualism stands."

"Laws never fit. . .corporations perfectly and will forever give rise to moral loopholes."

Stricter Penalties Would Not Reduce Corporate Crime

Thomas Donaldson

Thomas Donaldson is an associate professor in the Department of Philosophy at Loyola University in Chicago. A renowned educator, Mr. Donaldson's papers are published frequently by Notre Dame Press and the University of Maryland Press. He is the author of *Ethical Issues in Business, Corporations and Morality,* and *Case Studies in Business Ethics.* He is currently an officer in the Society for Business Ethics. In the following viewpoint, Mr. Donaldson discusses what he believes to be the ineffective manner in which laws govern corporations.

As you read, consider the following questions:

1. Why, according to the author, is it difficult to evaluate corporations for morality?
2. According to Mr. Donaldson, what are some of the difficulties with laws that prevent them from being real deterrents to corporate crime?
3. Does Mr. Donaldson seem to think that corporate behavior can be improved?

Thomas Donaldson, CORPORATIONS & MORALITY, © 1982, p14-15, 16, 17, 164-165, 166. Reprinted by permission of Prentice-Hall, Inc. Englewood Cliffs, N.J.

The task of moral theory is largely one of evaluation. But *can* the large modern corporation be conveniently evaluated alongside human beings? Can one evaluate a multinational giant as one would a person? When asking such questions it is worth remembering that the corporation is an amalgam of artifice and nature. That is, it is composed of natural human beings and reflects the natural tendency of humans to form organizations; but at the same time it is an artifact in the sense that it is a product of human intention and has a humanly malleable character. Unlike purely natural objects, we *decide*, up to a point, what the corporation is. We can grant or deny it unlimited longevity, limited liability, state citizenship, and so on. However, this makes the ethical task all the harder. Philosophically, we cannot fix the character of this abstract hybrid as we would an item in nature, such as a rock or tree, for part of what a corporation *is* is the product of our moral and legal imagination.

To be sure, some age-old questions facing the corporation are the same questions that confront individuals. St. Thomas Aquinas retells the story which Cicero presented in his *DE Officiis*, of the merchant confronted with a moral puzzle. The merchant is en route to a town stricken by famine, carrying grain to the starving townspeople. He knows, however, that other merchants are following him with more grain. Is he bound to tell the townspeople of the additional grain, or may he remain silent and command a higher price? Cicero concludes he must tell out of a sense of moral duty. Aquinas, however, reaches the opposite conclusion on the grounds that, although it would be commendable to tell, the merchant is not bound to predict a future event which, if it failed to occur, would rob him of a just price. The point is not whether one agrees with Cicero or Aquinas. The point is that regardless of the outcome, the moral issue is the same for corporations as it is for persons: namely, must corporations divulge information contrary to their interests when it would significantly benefit the consumer? . . .

Punishment for Moral Misdeeds

Other moral issues are less adaptable. Take the issue of the proper punishment for moral misbehavior. When an individual commits a crime, the punishment chosen applies to the entire person; we do not (except in barbaric systems) single out one part of the person, say his hand or eye. But when punishing a corporation, society frequently singles out a part of the corporation, say the board of directors, for special treatment.

Corporations thus present a fundamental ambiguity. For some purposes they may be treated as individuals; for others, not. The ambiguity is reflected in our psychological attitudes toward them. Leo Tolstoy writes that people's moral tolerance is greater for large organizations, especially legislatures, churches, and bureaucracies, than for individuals. Christopher Stone applies this idea to corporations. "If we are subjected to the noise of a motorcyclist driving up and down our street at night," Stone remarks, "I think a deeper and more complex level of anger is tapped in us than if we are subjected to the same disturbance (decibelly measured) from an airlines operation overhead.". . .

In stretching theories designed for individuals to cover corporations, one may also err by overlooking the economic mission of profit-making corporations. Whereas people exhibit a multitude of interests—friendship, money, love, and so on—corporations have exceedingly narrow personalities. They are chartered primarily for economic purposes and are designed for efficient economic production and little else. Where it may be a shortcoming for an individual to terminate his or her own existence or to be unmoved at the loss of an acquaintance, it is less clearly a flaw for a corporation. The corporation is an economic animal; although one may deny that its sole responsibility is to make a profit for its investors, one may nonetheless wish to define its responsibility differently than for individual humans. . . .

Ethical Punishment

"Recently, Chief Judge Warren K. Urbom, of the Federal District Court, in Lincoln, Nebraska, faced with sentencing the Missouri Valley Construction Company, of Grand Island, which had pleaded guilty to rigging state highway-construction bids in violation of the antitrust laws, decided that a fitting punishment would be to require the company to endow a chair of business ethics at the University of Nebraska. The judge went on to specify that the professor occupying the chair, which would yield an annual salary of around eighty thousand dollars, should be someone 'of national standing,' and that in his courses of instruction he should focus on business and professional ethics in general and bidding ethics in the engineering field in particular."

The New Yorker, August 29, 1983.

If present laws fail to guarantee good corporate behavior, why not press for new and tougher laws? Though such a step would fall short of ensuring perfect behavior, might it not succeed in raising the standards of corporations? Unfortunately, whatever the answer to these questions, there are deeper problems affecting the law's capacity to encourage morality and these reach to the very heart of law and morality.

No matter how legal mechanisms might be reconstructed, they

would need to be—as they always have been standardized and applied according to general rules. But because standardized formulas never fit all situations precisely, a margin of immoral but legally permissible behavior will remain. Consider the laws that confer special minority status upon blacks, American Indians, and people with Spanish surnames. In one instance, a white named Robert Earl Lee legally changed his name to "Roberto Eduardo," thus becoming eligible for minority status and, in turn, making it possible for a corporation to hire him and bolster its minority quota. Laws never fit either individuals or corporations perfectly and will forever give rise to moral loopholes.

Next there is the problem of the "negative" impact of law noted by moral philosophers such as St. Thomas Aquinas and Immanuel Kant. Laws tend to tell people what they ought *not* do, using negative terms, rather than telling people what they *should* do in positive ones. . . .

Concern for Employees

The law can specify minimum standards of acceptable behavior but it can do little to encourage wholehearted morality. It can attempt to force General Motors to install safety devices in cars, to monitor inplant pollutants, and to hire minorities, but it cannot force General Motors to develop a genuine concern for its employees and consumers.

Laws also suffer from their incapacity to anticipate the novel or unusual circumstance. They tend to be written in *response* to events rather than in *anticipation* of them. There is an inevitable time lag between the recognition of a problem and the law's capacity to control it, so the law always runs after moral problems and, like a man chasing to control it, so the law always runs after moral problems and, like the man chasing his coattails, can never quite catch them. Consider the introduction of laws controlling the packaging of meat and canned food products. The novelist Upton Sinclair, in his book *The Jungle*, exposed the horrors of the meat-packing industry when it was published in 1906: unsanitary conditions, diseased beef carcasses, and even instances of rats ground up in canned foods. But it was years before the law established effective controls through the Pure Food and Drug Administration. . . .

Even if the law could keep pace with the development of moral problems, certain problems would elude its grasp. Laws can frequently be effective in coercing reluctant corporate executives to remedy problems they otherwise would ignore. They are capable, for example, of forcing a company like Listerine to be cautious in the claims made in television ads and of demanding even that Listerine retract claims that its mouthwash "fights colds." Yet there exists an entirely different class of corporate abuses which the law is virtually helpless to prevent—namely, the problems that corporate executives themselves would eliminate if they only could. In a surprising number of corporate moral disasters, upper management is completely unaware of the events occurring at a lower level which prompt the disaster. Often, they would condemn the actions—if they only knew about them. Such problems stem from communication failures and entanglements of organizational structure. . . .

Conflict Between Efficiency and Regulation

Finally, there is the age-old conflict between efficiency and regulation; many of the business community's persistent complaints about regulation are valid. People who regulate cannot hope to have the necessary intimate acquaintance with a corporation's problems to impose restraints with maximum efficiency. The following scenario is all too common: An executive, a middle manager, or a craftsman, thoroughly familiar with the corporate operation he has worked years to perfect, is confronted with an outsider, perhaps from Washington, with little or no experience, who wishes to apply standardized rules to a nonstandard situation. Even when corporate executives sympathize with the goals of regulators, they can spot the clumsy, expensive, and inefficient "extras" which the regulators demand. Also, when regulatory agencies attempt to augment the experience of their staff by hiring people from the industry they regulate, they confront the dilemma of indoctrinating people schooled in anti-regulatory attitudes with pro-regulatory attitudes. . . .

All the difficulties of enforcing morality through law do not imply that regulation should be eliminated; however, they clearly expose significant limitations of the regulatory process. Encouraging and improving corporate moral behavior will require more than the external threats of the law.

"The need for controls should be instilled in the entire organization, starting with top management."

Better Management Policies Can Deter Computer Crime

Martin D. J. Buss and Lynn M. Salerno

Martin D. J. Buss is the director of planning for Philip Morris International. Prior to this he worked as a senior consultant to top management for Arthur D. Little, Inc. Lynn M. Salerno is associate editor of the *Harvard Business Review*. She is the editor of the *Harvard Business Review* collection *Catching Up with the Computer Revolution*. In the following viewpoint, the authors cite the drawbacks to current security methods. They believe that since no security measure is foolproof, the best deterrent to computer crime is better manager-employee relations.

As you read, consider the following questions:

1. Why do the authors consider people to be the weakest link in computer security?
2. What do the authors recommend to deter employees from committing computer crime?
3. Why do the authors consider computer hackers more amoral than immoral? Do you agree?

Recently we were treated to the spectacle of a 17-year-old youth advising congressmen on computer security. The young man was one of a group of teenagers who penetrated the computers of the Los Alamos National Laboratory in New Mexico and the Memorial Sloan-Kettering Cancer Center in New York City. These break-ins are just the most widely publicized instances of computer abuse, but they attracted attention because of the age of the perpetrators and the importance of the organizations they attacked.

As representatives from Los Alamos have emphasized that the high-school boys obtained no national security data and Sloan-Kettering has spoken only of monetary losses, these incursions might be viewed as just schoolboy pranks. Or are they cause for concern? Probably both. . . .

Security Solutions

As companies become aware of their increased vulnerability to computer crime, it is natural that demands arise for tougher laws and other measures to improve security. The most commonly advocated solutions to computer security problems, however, present difficulties themselves. . . .

Some companies now provide screening devices for network systems that call back users who seek to log on, thus verifying their legal access. And for data that travel over phone lines—the route most subject to interception—encryption devices exist that ·scramble the information during transit so that the receiver must decode it.

Though experts debate the security of these codes and some considered unbreakable have been broken, they generally serve their purpose. They are expensive, however, and while their prices are dropping, they are probably not worth using except for very sensitive data.

Predictable Passwords

In some companies the password that permits a user to enter the computer is taped to the side of the machine or is so predictable that a limited search will discover it. The young men who penetrated the Los Alamos and Sloan-Kettering computers had not targeted those particular systems. Like burglars, they roamed around until they found a window open in the form of an easily guessed password. As they later testified, manufacturers ship computers with an assigned password. Customers should change these, but a surprising number forget to.

Given this lax attitude, it is hardly surprising then that in many reported crimes, the perpetrators relied on boldness and found no barriers to entry. In one case, a Virginia man used his personal computer to get credit card numbers from a credit bureau. After he had charged $50,000 worth of goods by phone, he was caught when a United Parcel Service delivery man became suspicious about the many different names on the parcels he delivered to the same address.

It will probably be some time before the tension between the need for easy access and the need for security will be removed. In the meantime, however, many corporations have a long way to go before they must worry about this conflict. It also appears evident that, as in many other business problems, people are the weakest link. As IBM stated in a recent advertisement. "The computer didn't do it.". . .

Since computer activities take place in an internal control environment, substantive improvements in computer security will not occur unless the organization as a whole believes that internal control is important and sees evidence that a foundation of controls is in place to facilitate security. . . .

Elusive Subject

Part of the discomfort with computer security arises because it is an elusive subject. It does not seem as susceptible to managing as other business problems. While the details of computer security may be highly technical, there are nonetheless important elements that only senior managers can handle. These involve planning the organization of the security apparatus and setting the general security goals.

People Cause Computer Crime

It's not the computers that commit the crimes, and in most cases it's not the computers that make the errors. People cause the problems, so they must be involved in the solutions. First, employees who are put in contact with computers must be made sensitive to the responsibility they are being entrusted with. Second, employers must become more security-conscious.

Ken Huff, *People*, September 12, 1983.

In most companies responsibility for computer security is fragmented. It is also controversial, largely because many departments are involved, including data processing, security (guards and watchmen), insurance, personnel, audit, control, and risk management. But there is no designated worrier. The remedy is to appoint an executive to act as the focal point for all computer security-related issues. Indeed, some corporations have already recognized the dangers of the present muddled situation and have done just this. One of the leading Swiss banks, for example, has a manager who is responsible for security and international data flow issues.

The computer security executive should coordinate corporate security policies and activities and keep top management advised on important developments. He or she should devise a plan and budget for improving computer security; build a consensus as to what needs doing; participate in studies of risks; monitor relevant literature; lead major projects such as plans for disaster recovery, back-up, and the discovery of a major fraud; provide education and training in computer-related issues for the rest of the organization; and deal with other organizations and industry groups on issues of mutual concern. The computer security manager should have carte blanche to go anywhere, look into anything, and talk to anyone inside and outside the organization. . . .

Screening Computer Employees

Security ultimately depends on the people who use the computer. A determined villain will always defeat even the most sophisticated counter-measures that most corporations can afford. Personnel policies, then, become especially important.

Among the employees who pose a high security risk are systems and applications programmers, computer operators, and terminal users. For such people, hiring and screening procedures need to be especially rigorous. Ex-employees, even those who left on friendly terms, have been responsible for more than one computer fraud, sometimes in concert with their former workmates. Personal problems can have significant work implications, and drug abuse in particular is a serious risk. Unreasonably high living standards of low-ranking employees should ring warning bells. In one celebrated case, a junior programmer who, it turned out, had committed computer fraud, parked his shiny Mercedes next to the president's car in the parking lot for months without causing any inquiry.

On the positive side, high-risk employees also have high value and need greater protection as corporate assets. This may require special salary scales, improved benefits, an increased training budget, effective and sensitive grievance procedures for handling their complaints, and so forth.

Need for Controls

More than 15 years ago Joseph J. Wasserman stated in HBR that "no one group should bear complete responsibility for protecting the computer system. The need for controls should be instilled in the entire organization, starting with top management and extending to all personnel." The programs outlined in this article will help achieve this ideal—as fitting today as it was then.

In any event, though it merits the executive's close attention, computer security can never be absolute. And it may be part of a larger problem. As each day's newspaper reveals new and shocking details of crimes involving the computer, both business and society at large should ponder some of the wider issues only touched on here. They should consider, for example, whether we need broad legislation at the federal level to curb the activities of individuals and groups such as the young men who have been briefing congressional committees.

Calling themselves computer hackers or freaks (or "phreaks"), some young people clearly delight in their intrusions and in their expertise. Because of their interest in and knowledge of computers, they may very well enter companies as Information System professionals in a few years.

Their views toward their electronic depredations may be more amoral than immoral but, as some of our examples show, others seem to think the same way.

The prospects of dealing with this new group raise the question whether the climate that permits computer crime is part of a wider breakdown in ethical concerns. If the answer is yes, does the solution lie in education? Other problems, concerning privacy, responsibility, and a host of new relationships brought about by the computer, remain to be explored.

As the opportunities for computer abuse grow, with an increasing number of irresponsible actors ready to seize the advantages, companies and the public may have to drop a "gee-wiz" attitude toward computers—an attitude that may account not only for the colloquy between congressmen and computer freaks but also for the general inability to face the harder but necessary questions about computer use.

"There should be criminal statutes so clear and applicable that a potential perpetrator would have no excuse for not knowing that what he contemplated was a criminal offense."

Better Laws Can Deter Computer Crime

Donn B. Parker

Donn B. Parker, a former computer manager, is Senior Information Analyst at the Stanford Research Institute Information Science Laboratory. He has received several National Science Foundation Grants, and lectures throughout the US on computer criminals. A few of Mr. Parker's major works are *Crime by Computer, Ethical Conflicts in Computer Science and Technology,* and *Fighting Computer Crime.* In the followng viewpoint, Mr. Parker berates the lack of laws specifically outlining criminal computer activity. He believes that inadequate legislation is hampering the prosecution of computer crime.

As you read, consider the following questions:

1. Why does the author say that ethics alone are not effective against computer crime? Do you agree?
2. Does the author think that most computer criminals are unaware of wrongdoing? Why?
3. Does the author think that computer crime laws are lacking more at the state level or federal level?

Adherence to ethical principles can go only a short distance toward the protection of society from its miscreants; then the law must take over. Computer programmers in one computer center were routinely using their employer's computer for personal purposes. They had their bowling scores, church mailing lists, football pools, computer games, you name it in the computer. Management looked the other way and avoided the issue. It happens in hundreds of computer centers.

In this case two programmers were fooling around and discovered a means of automatically rescoring sheet music. A music company found out about it and started paying them money for running their program on their employer's computer. It looked as if it could be a successful business. They advertised and got more business and decided that, as soon as it reached a self-sustaining income, they would quit their jobs, form a company, buy computer services, and be off and running. In the meantime, the price of their service was based on free computer time.

One of the programmers told me they knew what they were doing was unethical but never dreamed that it was illegal. They were then facing prison sentences for mail fraud. Mail fraud! They stole computer services to the extent that their work occupied three-fourths of the entire storage capacity of the computer, and their managers were wondering why the computer jobs were queuing up and projects were falling behind. A disgruntled programmer jealous of the music scorers' business turned them in. But why were they convicted of mail fraud when they stole computer services?

In another case several computer maintenance engineers on strike sabotaged their employer's customer by playing a cassette recorder into a telephone with signals that caused punched paper tape devices in offices all over the country to spew whole reels of tape into hip-deep piles. They were convicted of the only law found to apply—a misdemeanor law normally used to convict obscene telephone callers. Where are the proper laws to fit these crimes? People should be convicted of the crimes they commit. There should be criminal statutes so clear and applicable that a potential perpetrator would have no excuse for not knowing that what he contemplated was a criminal offense.

Anatomy of a Computer Crime

My associate, Susan Nycum, one of the leading computer law attorneys in the world, investigated and documented the following interesting and significant case the occurred in 1975. Nycum published a paper on it in the *1978 National Computer Conference Proceedings*, most of which is reprinted here. The case is important for both legal and technical insights. A prosecutor said that it could not have been successfully prosecuted in his state because there were no laws that apply to the perpetrator's acts. Fortunately, the home where he performed the crime with a terminal and telephone was in another state, while the site of the computer was in the prosecutor's state. Therefore, the telephone line crossed a state boundary and the Federal Wire Fraud Statute prevailed.

This case was a theft of proprietary computer programs from a private computer installation over telephone lines. It was investigated by the FBI and prosecuted by a U.S. attorney, and the defendant pleaded not guilty. At a resulting jury trial the defendant was convicted on two counts, and one count was dismissed. The facts were typical of a particular form of abuse that had not been previously investigated in depth. . . .

The prosecutor stated that this had been the first exposure of that office to computer abuse, and they felt hampered by the lack of adequate federal law applicable to the case and by their own unfamiliarity with the type of activity. (The FBI could not be interviewed without a many months' delay because of a backlog of requests under the Freedom of Information Act. Their reports, however, had been used by the U.S. attorney, who did share his experience on the case with Nycum.)

Company Security Nonexistent

Security violations in networks happen all the time because security is virtually non-existent. "Businesses in the main are not giving one thought to anything—they're not really aware of the vulnerability."

Arielle Semmitt, *Personal Computing,* January 1984.

From the standpoint of programmers involved with programs developed other than by themselves entirely with their own resources, the case points out two critical matters.

Program Ownership

Most programs are owned by someone; few are actually in the public domain. If the perpetrator Brown thought himself innocent of any wrongdoing when he took a copy of the company program, he was woefully mistaken. That assumption, which fortunately is widespread, is wrong. Programmers must assume, unless assured otherwise by the persons responsible for the program, that it belongs to someone, and permission to copy or use the program must be obtained in advance of such use.

Computer security is a legitimate concern of all those involved with computers and programs. If Brown was truthful, his efforts to convince the company during his employment of its lack of systems security through memos and meetings were unsuccessful. His testimony was that, having failed to achieve better security while an employee of the company, Brown intended to copy the entire program after termination and present the company with the evidence of a series of perpetrations and the significant results of such accesses. (In fact, he accessed the system approximately sixty times without authority.) The jury disbelieved Brown. His case might have been stronger had those noble intentions been documented, or had he any way enunciated his concerns to users of the facility or to law enforcement personnel. Computer people whose personal ethics require action similar to Brown must realize and acknowledge that the action carries with it the possibility of conviction of a crime.

Computer Crimes Unreported

Unfortunately, it is a fact of life that business, as well as government, is reluctant to report computer crime. Several reasons account for this victim apathy: embarrassment, bad publicity, revelation of other questionable activity, stockholder lawsuits and having to report the crime to the Securities and Exchange Commission. Invariably, the losses are conveniently buried in one or more expense items.

Herchell Britton, *Vital Speeches of the Day,* June 1, 1981.

The case was interesting from a legal standpoint for several reasons. The judge's dismissal of the count of receipt of stolen property was the second time a jurist had been faced with the unauthorized transfer of a copy of a computer program in the form of electronic impulses over telephone lines. In both cases the judges found this act to be outside of the purview of the penal laws affecting asportation, or the carrying away, of personal property.

The prosecutors felt hampered in their conduct of the case by the lack of directly applicable law. They were fortunate that the alleged theft had been interstate and thereby subject to federal jurisdiction and the Federal Wire Fraud Statute. Had the incident occurred entirely intrastate, as stated at the beginning, the laws of the particular state involved might not have provided the source of a prosecutable offense.

The character of the property involved, a computer program, exposed the prosecution and the defense to the complicated and confusing issue of identification and protection of proprietary interests in programs.

Understanding Words in Context

Readers occasionally come across words which they do not recognize. And frequently, because the reader does not know a word or words, he or she will not fully understand the passage being read. Obviously, the reader can look up an unfamiliar word in a dictionary. However, by carefully examining the word in the context in which it is used, the word's meaning can often be determined. A careful reader may find clues to the meaning of the word in surrounding words, ideas and attitudes.

The excerpts below come primarily from the viewpoints in this chapter. In each excerpt, a word is printed in italics. Try to determine the meaning of each word by reading the excerpt. Under each excerpt you will find four definitions for the italicized word. Choose the one that is closest to your understanding of the word.

Finally, use a dictionary to see how well you have understood the words in context. It will be helpful to discuss with others the clues which helped you decide each word's meaning.

1. A less harsh remedy is to limit the charter of a company by preventing it from continuing those *ASPECTS* of criminal behavior.

   ASPECTS means
   a) phases
   b) honest acts
   c) techniques
   d) devious plots

2. Traditional criminals can be disabled if the society is willing to *COUNTENANCE* severe solutions.

   COUNTENANCE means
   a) disapprove
   b) approve
   c) reject
   d) forego

134

3. Disablement is more workable with corporate criminals because this kind of criminal activity is dependent on their being able to maintain legitimacy in formalized roles in the economy. Corporate crime's total dependence on *INCUMBENCY* of roles in the economy renders possible this tailor-made disablement.

   INCUMBENCY means
   a) frequency
   b) politicizing
   c) many levels
   d) organizing

4. A corporation could be forced to sell that part of its business which has been the *LOCUS* of continued law violation.

   LOCUS means
   a) instigator
   b) locality
   c) breeding ground
   d) beneficiary

5. Pickpockets can be *INCAPACITATED* by our cutting off their hands.

   INCAPACITATED means
   a) helped
   b) disabled
   c) benefitted
   d) encouraged

6. Corporations thus present a fundamental *AMBIGUITY*. For some purposes they may be treated as individuals; for others, not.

   AMBIGUITY means
   a) two-sided story
   b) criminal tendency
   c) clarity
   d) improvement

7. Laws can frequently be effective in *COERCING* reluctant corporate executives to remedy problems.

   COERCING means
   a) preventing
   b) helping
   c) pushing
   d) telling

8. There exists an entirely different class of corporate abuses which the law is *VIRTUALLY* helpless to prevent.

   VIRTUALLY means
   a) never
   b) almost always
   c) completely
   d) sometimes

9. There were no laws that apply to the *PERPETRATOR's* acts.

   PERPETRATOR means
   a) puppeteer   b) criminal
   c) gambler   d) executive

10. The computer program copied was a heavily modified *VARIANT* of a system.

    VARIANT means
    a) deviant   b) version
    c) section   d) main memory

11. The *COGNIZANT* U.S. attorney prosecuted the perpetrator for violation of federal law.

    COGNIZANT means
    a) senior   b) attractive
    c) mindful   d) honest

12. These *INCURSIONS* might be viewed as just schoolboy pranks.

    INCURSIONS means
    a) status offenses   b) break-ins
    c) theft by computer d) juvenile crime

13. Given this *LAX* attitude, it is hardly surprising then that in many reported crimes, the perpetrators relied on boldness.

    LAX means
    a) relaxed   b) wonderful
    c) stupid   d) cowardly

14. A foundation of controls is in place to *FACILITATE* security.

    FACILITATE means
    a) service   b) increase dramatically
    c) make easier   d) prevent

15. Part of the discomfort with computer security arises because it is an *ELUSIVE* subject.

    ELUSIVE means
    a) embarrassing   b) difficult
    c) technical   d) evasive

Bibliography

The following list of periodical articles deals with the subject matter of this chapter.

Charles Alexander	"Crackdown on Computer Capers," *Time*, February 8, 1982.
August Bequai	"Crime That Pays," *New York Times*, April 19, 1984.
Herchell Britton	"The Serious Threat of White-Collar Crime: What Can You Do? *Vital Speeches of the Day*, June 1, 1981.
David Burnham	"Loophole in the Law Raises Concern about the Privacy in the Computer Age," *New York Times*, December 19, 1983.
Business Week	"A New Weapon against Labor Racketeers," February 14, 1983.
Business Week	"Can a Racketeering Law Be Applied to Brokers?" January 10, 1983.
Christopher Byron	"Big Profits in Big Bribery," *Time*, March 16, 1981.
David Cherrington, W. Stevens Albrect Marshall B. Romney	"Fighting White-Collar Crime—What Managers Can Do," *Working Woman*, February 1982.
Robert Elias	"Crimes That Don't Count," *The Progressive*, September 1981.
Lee Gomes	"Secrets of the Software Pirates," *Esquire*, January 1982.
Peter Large	"Coping With Computer Crime," *World Press Review*, July 1981.
William McGowan	"The Great White-Collar Crime Coverup," *Business and Social Review*, Spring 1983.
Dorothy J. Samuels	"Privacy Vs. Computers," *New York Times*, September 12, 1983.
Robert C. Soloman and Others	"The Case Against Corporate Virtue," *Esquire*, January 1982.
Sidney C. Sufrin	"How Moral Can a Business Be?" *The Christian Century*, March 2, 1983.

Would Gun Control
Reduce Crime?

*"People **with** guns do the most robbing and killing in the United States."*

Three Arguments for Gun Control

Edward F. Dolan Jr.

Edward F. Dolan Jr. is an author whose writing covers a broad range of subjects. His published works include *Amnesty: The American Puzzle, Adolf Hilter, Child Abuse,* and several books in the field of sports. The following viewpoint is excerpted from his book *Gun Control,* which deals with the criminal, social, and economic aspects of the controversial issue of gun control in America. In it, Mr. Dolan presents three pro-gun control arguments: that a handgun is a poor defensive weapon, that gun control will prevent crimes of passion, and that strict gun control measures have been proven to reduce crime.

As you read, consider the following questions:

1. According to the author, why is a handgun a poor defensive weapon?
2. Why does Mr. Dolan believe that gun control will prevent crimes of passion?
3. How does the homicide rate in Great Britain compare with homicides in the US?

One of the main anti-control arguments is that, when criminals know that someone can handle a gun, they are far less willing to make him or her their victim. . . .

The Pro-Control Argument: *A handgun is a very poor defensive weapon.* You need only look to a 1973 study to see that a gun is too dangerous a weapon to be kept around the house for self-protection. The study, made by two Ohio coroners and two professors from Case Western Reserve University, shows that:

A gun kept for protection is six times more likely to kill someone you know rather than an attacker. Seventy percent of the people killed by handguns are shot by relatives or acquaintances.

The same warning has come from the National Commission on the Causes and Prevention of Violence, which was formed in 1968 by President Lyndon B. Johnson. The commission reported that, for every burglar stopped by a gun, four gun owners or members of their families are killed in firearms accidents.

The National Council for the Control of Handguns points to yet another danger. For the most part, the gun is actually useless as a defense against burglars because 90 percent of all housebreaks are committed when the tenants are away. The gun is among the items usually stolen. It then makes its way into the underworld and contributes to the increase of crime and violence in the nation. . . .

In all, it's nonsense to say that the gun protects. Rather, it injures or kills innocent people in accidental and mistaken shootings. And it is too likely to be stolen and passed into the underworld.

The Gun and Crime

Anti-control supporters contend that tough laws against the gun will not reduce crime and violence in the United States. They put their argument in the simplest of terms: The gun by itself doesn't kill or commit some other crime. People do. So act against the gunman, not the gun.

The pro-control camp agrees that, by itself, the gun doesn't kill. But they point out that people *with* guns do the most robbing and killing in the United States. . . .

The Pro-Control Argument: *Maybe gun control won't keep guns out of the hands of criminals, but it will prevent crimes of passion.* We agree that the handgun is harmless until someone picks it up. But, once held in the human hand, it becomes the weapon *most often* used in crime and the weapon *most responsible* for murders in this country. . . .

Most handgun murders in the United States are not committed by criminals. Rather, as the FBI reported in 1975, almost 70 percent of the country's murders were committed by family

Reprinted by permission of United Features Syndicate.

members or acquaintances. FBI statistics in 1980 showed these figures to be down to 51 percent. These murders are known as "crimes of passion" because they occur when someone so loses his temper during a flare-up that he grabs a gun in a blind rage.

Why is the handgun such a popular murder weapon? Basically because, from the killer's standpoint, it is a "safe" weapon. It can be fired at a distance. The assailant need not have bodily contact with his victim and run the risk of injury to himself, as would be the case if he picked up a baseball bat or tried to settle things with his fists. And it's deadly; the person who is shot isn't likely to get up off the floor and attack the gunman.

There's only one way to stop the senseless "crimes of passion"—and that's to remove the handgun from reach. Then it won't be readily at hand when someone flies into a rage. He'll have to think twice before attacking. He'll have to find another weapon. All this will give him the time to cool down. A life will be saved.

These same facts work for suicide. A person about to take his life might have the time to reconsider if he can't simply walk to a bureau drawer and take out a gun. And nothing needs to be said about the accidents that will be prevented once the handgun is out of reach.

Now let's turn from the ordinary citizen to the actual criminal. The causes of crime and violence in our society are many and complex. To cite just two, there is, first, the rapid growth of our cities, which is throwing millions of people together in crowded and uncomfortable circumstances. And there is the sad fact that so many of our people have so much money and so many advantages while just as many of our people are forced to live in poverty, held there by such factors as racial discrimination and poor educational opportunities.

If crime and violence are to be reduced, these problems and many others must be solved. Strong and firmly enforced laws against the criminal, as helpful as they can be, won't do the whole job. But it's going to take years to solve these problems—perhaps even several generations. Controls against the handgun, however, can be swiftly enacted and can do much to cut down on crime and violence in the meantime. The controls can the go right on doing an effective job after the problems have been partially or totally solved.

One Fewer Killing

I know that gun-control is an imperfect solution. But I know, too, that the only reason to have a gun is to kill, and if gun-control rids this world of just one gun, there might just be one fewer killing. Maybe a doctor could continue to cure, or a bartender mix drinks, or a mother see her grandchildren, or John Lennon write another song.

Richard Cohen, *Washington Post,* December 14, 1980.

It must also be remembered that strong laws against the criminal will do nothing to prevent "crimes of passion." There is no law that can keep a man from flying into a rage. Only strong controls, putting the handgun out of his reach, can take care of things.

Do Gun Laws Really Work?

This is one of the most hotly argued questions in the whole debate.

Pro-control supporters do not believe the opposition's argument that future controls won't work because the criminal won't obey them. They contend that, whenever U.S. cities have enacted tough control laws and then enforced them, the murder rates there have dropped. Further, all foreign nations with strict controls have lower crime rates than we; it's time that we learned a lesson from them.

The anti-control camp answers that, in many cities with strong gun laws, the murder rates have actually gone up. So far as other countries are concerned, the controls have little to do with the low crime rates there. Crime rates in other nations depend more on the nature of the people and their traditions than on control laws.

The Pro-Control Argument: *Areas with strict gun control have lower crime rates than areas with loose controls.* The recent experiences of two large American cities have proved how effective controls can be. The cities are Philadelphia, Pennsylvania, and Toledo, Ohio.

Alarmed at its crime rate, Philadelphia in 1965, passed a law requiring every citizen to furnish the police department with fingerprints and a photograph when obtaining a permit to buy a gun. In one year alone, the law exposed twenty-seven applicants who had once been convicted on "intent-to-kill" charges; sixty-nine with past records for carrying concealed weapons; and close to 200 with robbery, theft, rape, and narcotics addiction records. While firearms are now responsible for 66 percent of the murders committed in America, they are responsible only 58 percent of the time in Philadelphia.

Stopping the Carnage

It's time to stop the carnage. We must have federal handgun registration. This nation requires the registration of automobiles and tests the skills of drivers, but does nothing to check on who owns or uses handguns. . . .

Must other children, other wives, other husbands die? Must another leader be assassinated? Surely enough have died already. Let's begin now to get rid of the weapons that make it so easy to blow our loved ones away.

John C. Quinn, *USA Today*, April 4, 1984.

In 1968, Toledo passed a similar law. Two years later, the handgun murder rate in the city that was once known as "the gun capital of the midwest" had dropped twenty-two percentage points. Need more be said?

Now for foreign countries: Starting with Great Britain, the homicide rates speak for themselves.

The rate in England and Wales in the early 1970s, for instance, stood at an astonishingly low 0.04 people per 100,000 population; the rate for Scotland was 0.1. In 1971, with a population of about 50 million, England and Wales had only 35 homicides with firearms, while the United States, with 207 million people, had 12,243 such killings—or about eighty-five times as many. London reported only 2 handgun murders in 1972.

Great Britain requires that every citizen receive a certificate of competence before buying or owning a gun. The British feel that their low homicide rates are due to the fact that the authorities have been successful in keeping people from carrying "offensive weapons" and have punished those who don't obey the laws.

The murder rate in Japan is even lower than in Great Britain. It stood at 0.02 per 100,000 population in the late 1960s. During 1972, this island country of 107 million people had only 28 handgun murders; the United States suffered 10,017 handgun slayings that year. The city of Tokyo reported only 3 handgun murders in 1970 and only one in 1971.

Japan completely outlaws the possession of handguns by private citizens.

Great Britain and Japan are not just isolated examples. . . .

In France, anyone who plans to buy a gun must first undergo an intensive police investigation. The Netherlands requires a permit for all firearms. In Australia, all shotguns and .22 rifles must be registered; pistols and rifles must be registered and their owners must have licenses.

In addition, there are five European countries that, like Japan, totally prohibit the private ownership of handguns. They are Albania, Cyprus, Greece, Ireland, and the Soviet Union.

Gun-control laws have all worked to reduce crime in these countries. They can do the same for us.

144

"Were gun controllers to succeed in eliminating the private possession of handguns, the end result might be a quadrupling of the homicide rate."

Three Myths of Gun Control

Don Feder

Don Feder is the editor of *On Principle*, a newsletter that presents arguments founded on the "primacy of reason, the sovereignty of the individual, and the efficacy of the free market." The following viewpoint is excerpted from an article he authored for this newsletter. In it, Mr. Feder explains why he believes that the three gun control arguments in the previous viewpoint are myths.

As you read, consider the following questions:

1. Why does the author call the first argument for gun control his "favorite myth"?
2. Does Mr. Feder think that gun control will prevent crimes of passion? Do you agree?
3. How does the author dispute foreign comparisons of gun control and crime?

Don Feder, "Seven Myths of Gun Control," originally published in the May 16, 1983 issue of *On Principle*, a biweekly newsletter from a free-market point of view. *On Principle*, Princeton Professional Park, Suite B-7, 601 Ewing St., Princeton, NJ 08542.

Myth #1—*A handgun is a very poor defensive weapon.* This is commonly stated as one of my favorite myths of gun control: A gun in the house is 6 times more likely to kill a friend or family member as an intruder.

Fact—This amazing "statistic" is based on a study of homicides in Cleveland, Ohio from 1958 to 1973. No distinction was made between handguns and long-arms. Suicides were lumped in with accidental deaths and crimes of passion. More importantly, the study was simply a comparison of the number of intruders killed by homeowners with the number of family members who died via a household gun. There was no consideration of the criminals captured, wounded or driven off by armed homeowners, a far larger number than those killed outright.

With adequate training, a handgun can be employed quite effectively for self-defense. In a 1977 California poll, 8.6% of the gun owners responding said they'd used a handgun to defend themselves, their homes or their families, in the past five years. A 1978 survey by Patrick Cadell's Cambridge Research Reports, commissioned by an anti-gun group (the Center for the Study of Handgun Violence), projected that 300,000 Americans use a handgun each year to deter crime.

In Chicago, police have kept records of justifiable homicides by civilians for the past 40 years. In each of those years, the number of criminals dispatched by citizens has exceeded the number killed by police. In the past 5 years, 3 times as many robbers and intruders were killed by civilians as by the Chicago police.

Lastly, in a 1976 survey of the nation's leading law enforcement officials, conducted by the Boston Police Department, 80% of the law officers responding were of the opinion that individuals could effectively use a handgun for the defense of person or property. Indeed, every national police organization supports civilian ownership of handguns, including: The International Association of Chiefs of Police, the National Sheriffs Association and the National Police Officers Association of America. . . .

Myth #2—*Maybe gun control won't keep guns out of the hands of criminals, but it will prevent crimes of passion.*

Fact—"Crimes of passion" refers to the murder of friends and family members, committed "in the heat of anger." The crimes of passion argument is based on two erroneous assumptions about these homicides.

First, it is assumed that the average citizen will obey gun laws. Historical experience contradicts this assumption. In 1911, New York City enacted the Sullivan Law, which required the registration and licensing of firearms. Today, after 70 years of Sullivan, the police estimate there are one to two million illegal handguns in the City. It's a safe bet that the vast majority of those guns are not in the hands of criminals.

In 1977, the District of Columbia passed an ordinance requiring the registration of firearms and prohibiting the possession of unregistered weapons. Approximately 22,000 guns were duly registered. However, based on estimates of per capita gun ownership in metropolitan areas, there are probably 100,000 firearms in the D.C.—78% of which are unregistered.

The second fallacy of the crimes of passion argument is that if a handgun isn't present in the home, the crime will somehow be thwarted. But what if long-arms (rifles or shotguns) are substituted for pistols in the commission of these crimes? There are approximately twice as many long-arms in private hands in this country as handguns. While the mortality rate for handgun wounds is only 5 to 10%, with rifle and shotgun wounds, 30-40% are fatal. In other words, were gun controllers to succeed in eliminating the private possession of handguns, the end result might be a quadrupling of the homicide rate.

If the presence of a gun in the home does increase the likelihood of family killings, then it's logical to assume that an increase in gun ownership will result in more gun slayings. In fact, just the opposite is true. Between 1974 and 1979, firearms

Bob Dix, *Manchester Union Leader.* Reprinted with permission.

involvement in all violent crimes fell 14%. The firearm murder rate declined 9%; the firearm assault rate dropped 17%. During the same period, Americans purchased an additional 10-12 million handguns and 20-22 million rifles and shotguns.

Who commits crimes of passion? Gun controllers would have us believe it's ordinary people. Joe Milk Toast comes home one Friday evening, drinks too much, and shoots his nagging wife. Crime statistics refute this stereotype. Two-thirds of those arrested for interfamilial homicides have prior arrest records for violent felonies. In 90% of family killings, the police have been called to the home on at least one prior occassion to break up a violent argument. In over half the cases, police have been to the home five or more times, prior to the killing. In other words, the average perpetrator of a crime of passion is a violent sociopath—just the type of person least likely to obey gun laws. . . .

Myth #3—*Areas with strict gun control have lower crime rates than areas with loose controls.* This myth is is often posed in terms of foreign comparisons; i.e.: look at how well gun control has worked in Great Britain.

Fact—Twenty percent of all homicides in this country occur in 4 cities with just 6% of the population—New York, Chicago, Detroit and Washington, D.C. All have strict gun control.

According to the FBI's Uniform Crime Reports for 1979, of the 15 states with the highest homicide rates, 10 have restrictive or very restrictive gun laws.

In 1976, Massachusetts passed the notorious Bartley-Fox law, which provides a mandatory year in jail for carrying an unlicensed handgun. At that time, Massachusetts was the 19th most violent state and Boston the 5th most violent large city (based on a per capita average of all violent crimes—murder, rape, armed robbery and assault). In 1981, after 5 years of Bartley-Fox, Massachusetts had moved up to the 11th most violent state. Boston was the most violent major metropolitan area.

Gun controllers are forever touting Britain's low crime rate. They want you to believe that England's crime rate is a direct result of its gun laws. Of course, they neglect to mention that Britain had an even lower crime rate in the 1920's, prior to the imposition of any type of gun control. While Britain may currently have a low crime rate per capita, relative to the U.S. England's murder rate is growing by leaps and bounds. Between 1930 and 1975, the U.S. homicide rate rose 30%. From 1960 to 1975, the British murder rate doubled.

Gun prohibitionists tend to focus on foreign examples which support their thesis, and ignore the rest. For instance, the four countries with the highest per capita gun ownership—Switzerland, Israel, Denmark and Finland—all have relatively low crimes rates. Taiwan, which bans the private ownership of handguns, has a homicide rate twice that of the U.S.

In 1974, Jamaica outlawed the private ownership of all firearms and ammunition. Possession of a single bullet was punishable by life in prison. In 1980, after 6 years of this Draconian gun prohibition, Jamaica had 6 times as many gun deaths per capita as Washington, D.C.—one of the most violent cities in America.

"People kill people, but handguns make it easier."

The Case for Gun Control

Adam Smith

Adam Smith is a prominent journalist. His editorial column, "Unconventional Wisdom" appears regularly in issues of *Esquire*, a sophisticated men's magazine. As an author, he has addressed many topical issues in his books which include *The Money Game*, *Supermoney*, *Powers of Mind*, and *Paper Money*. In the following viewpoint, Mr. Smith argues that rather than deterring crime, citizen ownership of guns contributes to criminal violence.

As you read, consider the following questions:

1. How does the author describe the "gun culture"?
2. What are some of Mr. Smith's antigun arguments?
3. How does the author think that registry of handguns would decrease the crime rate?

Adam Smith, "Fifty Million Handguns," *Esquire*, April 1981. Reprinted with permission from Esquire. Copyright © 1981 by Esquire Associates.

"You people," said my Texas host, "do not understand guns or gun people." By "you people" he meant not just me, whom he happened to be addressing, but anyone from a large eastern or midwestern city. My Texas host is a very successful businessman, an intelligent man. "There are two cultures," he said, "and the nongun culture looks down on the gun culture."

My Texas host had assumed—correctly—that I do not spend a lot of time with guns. The last one I knew intimately was a semi-automatic M-14, and, as any veteran knows, the army bids you call it a weapon, not a gun. I once had to take that weapon apart and reassemble it blindfolded, and I liked it better than the heavy old M-1. We were also given a passing introduction to the Russian Kalashnikov and the AK-47, the Chinese copy of that automatic weapon, presumably so we could us these products of our Russian and Chinese enemies if the need arose. I remember that you could drop a Kalashnikov in the mud and pick it up and it would still fire. I also remember blowing up a section of railroad track using only an alarm clock, a primer cord, and a plastic called C-4. The day our little class blew up the track at Fort Bragg was rather fun. These experiences give me some credibility with friends from the "gun culture." (Otherwise, they have no lasting social utility whatsoever.) And I do not share the fear of guns—at least of "long guns," rifles and shotguns—that some of my college-educated city-dweller friends have, perhaps because of my onetime intimacy with that Army rifle, whose serial number I still know.

The Gun Culture

In the gun culture, said my Texas host, a boy is given a .22 rifle around the age of twelve, a shotgun at fourteen, and a .30 caliber rifle at sixteen. The young man is taught to use and respect these instruments. My Texas host showed me a paragraph in a book by Herman Kahn in which Kahn describes the presentation of the .22 as a rite of passage, like a confirmation or a bar mitzvah. "Young persons who are given guns," he wrote, "go through an immediate maturing experience because they are thereby given a genuine and significant responsibility." Any adult from the gun culture, whether or not he is a relative, can admonish any young person who appears to be careless with his weapon. Thus, says Kahn, the gun-culture children take on "enlarging and maturing responsibilities" that their coddled upper-middle-class counterparts from the nongun culture do not share. The children of my Texas host said "sir" to their father and "ma'am" to their mother.

I do not mean to argue with the rite-of-passage theory. I am quite willing to grant it. I bring it up because the subjects of guns and gun control are very emotional ones, and if we are to solve the problems associated with them, we need to arrive at a consensus within and between gun and nongun cultures in our country.

Please note that the rite-of-passage gifts are shotguns and rifles. Long guns have sporting uses. Nobody gives a child a handgun, and nobody shoots a flying duck with a .38 revolver. Handguns have only one purpose.

Steve Sack, *Minneapolis Star and Tribune*. Reprinted with permission.

Some months ago, a college friend of mine surprised a burglar in his home in Washington, D.C. Michael Halberstam was a cardiologist, a writer, and a contributor to this magazine. The burglar shot Halberstam, but Halberstam ran him down with his car on the street outside before he died, and the case received widespread press. I began to work on this column, in high anger, right after his death. A few days later, John Lennon was killed in New York. These two dreadful murders produced an outpouring of grief, followed immediately by intense anger and the demand that something be done, that Congress pass a gun-control law. The National Rifle Association was quick to point out that a gun-contol law would not have prevented either death; Halberstam's killer had already violated a whole slew of existing laws, and Lennon's was clearly sufficiently deranged or determined to kill him under any gun law. The National Rifle Association claims a million members, and it is a highly organized lobby. Its Political Victory Fund "works for the defeat of antigun candidates and for the support and election of progun office seekers." Let us grant the National Rifle Association position that the accused killers in these two recent spectacular shootings might not have been deterred even by severe gun restrictions.

In the course of researching this column, I talked to representatives of both the progun and the antigun lobbies. Anomalies abound. Sam Fields, a spokesman for the National Coalition to Ban Handguns, is an expert rifleman who was given a gun at age thirteen by his father, a New York City policeman. The progun banner is frequently carried by Don Kates Jr., who describes himself as a liberal, a former civil rights workers, and a professor of constitutional law. Fields and Kates have debated each other frequently. Given their backgrounds, one might expect their positions to be reversed.

Some of the progun arguments run as follows:

Guns don't kill people, people kill people. Gun laws do not deter criminals. (A 1976 University of Wisconsin study of gun laws concluded that "gun-control laws have no individual or collective effect in reducing the rate of violent crime.") A mandatory sentence for carrying an unlicensed gun, says Kates, would punish the "ordinary decent citizens in high-crime areas who carry guns illegally because police protection is inadequate and they don't have the special influence necessary to get a 'carry' permit." There are fifty million handguns out there in the United States already; unless you were to use a giant magnet, there is no way to retrieve them. The majority of people do not want guns banned. A ban on handguns would be like Prohibition—widely disregarded, unenforceable, and corrosive to the nation's sense of moral order. Federal registration is the beginning of federal tyranny; we might someday need to use those guns against the government.

Some of the antigun arguments go as follows:

People kill people, but handguns make it easier. When other weapons (knives, for instance) are used, the consequences are not so often deadly. Strangling or stabbing someone takes a different degree of energy and intent than pulling a trigger. Registration will not interfere with hunting and other rifle sports but will simply exercise control over who can carry handguns. Ordinary people do not carry handguns. If a burglar has a gun in his hand, it is quite insane for you to shoot it out with him, as if you were in a quick-draw contest in the Wild West. Half of all the guns used in crimes are stolen; 70 percent of the stolen guns are handguns. In other words, the supply of handguns used by criminals already comes to a great extent from the households these guns were supposed to protect.

A Tragic Loss of Life

The only way to prevent the tragic loss of life—the 32,000 lives a year that we're losing to handguns—is to say: "We no longer need handguns. They serve no valid purpose, except to kill people.". . .

People tend not to perceive handguns to be a problem to them personally. They think that handgun deaths are something that happens to other people. It has not come home to us yet that those 32,000 people who are dying each year are our friends and our neighbors. It's much easier to take a live-and-let-live stance.

Michael Beard, *U.S. News & World Report*, December 22, 1980.

"I'll tell you one thing," said a lieutenant on the local police force in my town. "You should never put that decal in your window, the one that says THIS HOUSE IS PROTECTED BY AN ARMED CITIZEN. The gun owners love them, but that sign is just an invitation that says 'Come and rob my guns.' Television sets and stereos are fenced at a discount; guns can actually be fenced at a premium. The burglar doesn't want to meet you. I have had a burglar tell me, 'If I wanted to meet people, I would have been a mugger.'"

Danger of Accidents

After a recent wave of burglaries, the weekly newspaper in my town published a front-page story. "Do not buy a gun—you're more likely to shoot yourself than a burglar," it said. At first the police agreed with that sentiment. Later, they took a slightly different line. "There is more danger from people having accidents or their kids getting hold of those guns than any service in

154

defending their houses; but there was a flap when the paper printed that, so now we don't say anything," said my local police lieutenant. "If you want to own a gun legally, okay. Just be careful and know the laws.

What police departments tell inquiring citizens seems to depend not only on the local laws but also on whether or not that particular police department belongs to the gun culture.

Some of the crime statistics underlying the gun arguments are surprising. Is crime-ridden New York City the toughest place in the country? No: your chances of being murdered are higher in Columbus, Georgia, in Pine Bluff, Arkansas, and in Houston, Texas, among others. Some of the statistics are merely appalling: we had roughly ten thousand handgun deaths last year. The British had forty. In 1978, there were 18,714 Americans murdered. Sixty-four percent were killed with handguns. In that same year, *we had more killings with handguns by children ten years old and younger than the British had by killers of all ages.* The Canadians had 579 homicides last year; we had more than twenty thousand.

Violence and Apple Pie

H. Rap Brown, the Sixties activist, once said, "Violence is as American as apple pie." I guess it is. We think fondly of Butch Cassidy and the Sundance Kid; we do not remember the names of the trainmen and the bank clerks they shot. Four of our Presidents have died violently; the British have never had a prime minister assassinated. *Life* magazine paid $8,000 to Halberstam's accused killer for photos of his boyhood. Now he will be famous, like Son of Sam. The list could go on and on.

I am willing to grant to the gunners a shotgun in every closet. Shotguns are not used much in armed robberies, or even by citizens in arguments with each other. A shotgun is a better home-defense item anyway, say my police friends, if only because you have to be very accurate with a handgun to knock a man down with one. But the arguments over which kinds of guns are best only demonstrate how dangerously bankrupt our whole society is in ideas on personal safety.

Our First Lady has a handgun.

World Registry of Handguns

Would registry of handguns stop the criminal from carrying the unregistered gun? No, and it might afflict the householder with some extra red tape. However, there is a valid argument for registry. Such a law might have no immediate effect, but we have to begin somewhere. We license automobiles and drivers. That does not stop automobile deaths, but surely the highways would be even more dangerous if populated with unlicensed drivers and uninspected cars. The fifty million handguns outstanding have not caused the crime rate to go down. Another two million handguns will be sold this year, and I will bet that the crime rate still does not go down.

Our national behavior is considered close to insane by some of the other advanced industrial nations. We have gotten so accustomed to crime and violence that we have begun to take them for granted; thus we are surprised to learn that the taxi drivers in Tokyo carry far more than five dollars in cash, that you can walk safely around the streets of Japan's largest cities, and that Japan's crime rate is going *down*. I know there are cultural differences; I am told that in Japan the criminal is expected to turn himself in so as not to shame his parents. Can we imagine that as a solution to crime here?

In a way, the tragic killings of Michael Halberstam and John Lennon have distracted us from a larger and more complex problem. There is a wave of grief, a wave of anger—and then things go right on as they did before. We become inured to the violence and dulled to the outrage. Perhaps, indeed, no legislation could stop murders like these, and perhaps national gun legislation would not produce overnight change. The hard work is not just to get the gunners to join in; the hard work is to do something about our ragged system of criminal justice, to shore up our declining faith in the institutions that are supposed to protect us, and to promote the notion that people should take responsibility for their own actions.

What makes us so different from the Japanese and the British and the Canadians? They are not armed, as we are, yet their streets and houses are far safer. Should we not be asking ourselves some sober questions about whether we are living the way we want to?

"The way we see it, if they have the right to mug us, we have the right to shoot them."

The Case Against Gun Control

Chip Elliot

Chip Elliot is a novelist now living in the Midwest. A former advertising agency writer, he received his education at Stanford University and resided in the San Francisco and Los Angeles areas of California prior to his move to the Midwest. In the following viewpoint, Mr. Elliot makes use of his own case history to dramatically illustrate his argument in favor of the use of guns for self-defense.

As you read, consider the following questions:

1. What situation prompted the author to purchase a gun?
2. Do you think that the author's gun keeps him from becoming victimized?
3. Why does the author think that owning a gun is a good deterrent against crime?

Chip Elliot, "The Case for Guns," *Esquire*, June 1983. Reprinted by permission of the author.

We are living in a world where personal self-defense is a necessity. . . .

I went from [nonacceptance] to carrying a 9mm Smith & Wesson automatic in ten weeks. My wife is a psychiatrist. Very attractive, very easy to intimidate, very abstracted, a likely target for muggers both outside, because she's lost in her thoughts, and at home, because punks think doctors keep drugs in their houses (they don't). She has a gun, too, a .38, and she knows how to use it. We are not hillbillies: we are people who went to Radcliffe and Stanford, respectively. Appalling, huh? It used to appall us too, until we were forced to realize that our lives, both as a married couple with a deep commitment and as individuals doing important and meaningful work, were *worth protecting.*

In the spring of 1976 we were living in the San Francisco Bay area. My wife was doing her psychiatric residency. I had just walked out on the advertising business and was working on a novel. . . .

Living by the Sea

Two years later, we moved to Los Angeles. We did not move to the glamorous, movie-struck Los Angeles of The Ginger Man and the Beverly Hill Hotel—though I would by lying if I said the thought had never crossed our minds. We moved to the Los Angeles of the Nuart theater, the Fox Venice, the Jung Institute, a city with the sense of being in another country with American hamburger overtones. And, of course, the sea. Not the beach, the sea.

Our friends Boris and Ute—a Yugoslav sculptor and a German painter—had just bought a house in Venice, and we quickly rented a house nearby on Electric Avenue. Electric Avenue yet! *Whooee!* It was dirty pink with a gray-green roof, and its outstanding feature was an eight-by-thirty glassed-in porch. A grown man in good condition could have torn this house down with his hands, but I loved it because it swayed when you walked through it. It was like being on a weather-beaten but seaworthy closed-cabin schooner.

Venice at that time seemed like Sleeping Beauty after a century of trance: musty, dusty, and long stagnant, but with the promise of awakening magic. On that porch I intended to write a new *Threepenny Opera*, to invent at least two or three new Sally Bowleses. I would knock the world on its ear.

More Friends

More friends quickly turned up: Rene and Renata, European graphic wizards; Carolyn and Chris, a mime and an actor who wanted to get away from off-Broadway and into movies and television; a middle-aged Australian writer and adventurer and his half-Irish-half-Mexican wife with her wall-to-wall cheekbones and her head full of D. H. Lawrence and Denise Levertov. . .and many others.

My beloved French Lop rabbit, Nicole, had a yard to romp in. We quickly discovered a sensational wine from a local vineyard, a county-fair prizewinner that sold for $3.38 a *gallon* at the local Safeway.

Our days quickly became ordered: group breakfasts, work all day, talk all evening, lights out ten p.m. My wife took a job as staff psychiatrist for a county mental-health clinic in downtown Los Angeles. We settled in in a hurry. There was no time to lose. We were going to re-create the world not of the Sixties but of F. Scott Fitzgerald's friends Gerald and Sara Murphy in the years 1922 and 1923. We would throw a two-year-long working party.

But it quickly became apparent that all was not as it seemed in Venice. . . .

The Problem Is Violence

The problem in American society is violence, not handguns. Blaming crime on handguns is like blaming wet streets for rain. To use handguns as a facile explanation for our high crime rate is to ally oneself with those who believe that our social environment is to blame for violence. For their actions, that blame lies with the environment. If we just restructure the environment, these utopians say—just remove the handguns and other unpleasant items—society will be more harmonious. Nonsense.

Mark W. Hendrickson, *New Guard*, Summer 1982.

One morning, as I was sitting on the wobbly glassed-in porch, I watched a gang of black teenagers pour gasoline all over a parked car and set it on fire. This was at ten o'clock in the morning. Broad daylight.

A few days later, I heard of a robbery two blocks from where we lived: A woman came to the door of a house and asked to use the telephone, said it was an emergency. When the man opened the door, her henchmen came in right behind her. The three of them stabbed the man to death and left his wife barely alive. In the next block a woman was raped twice after her nose and jaw were broken.

Just to be on the safe side, after a kitchen-table powwow, we went to a gun shop on Pico Boulevard one Saturday morning and bought a .38 snub-nosed revolver. After all, this *was* Los Angeles, land of Joe Friday. Strange things had happened here. Sharon Tate had once had a very bad evening here. But a gun! Who had ever owned a gun? I picked the revolver up after the normal fifteen-day waiting period and wrote the guy a check from the Santa Monica Bank. It cost $160. It seemed like a lot for a silly object. I would rather have bought a painting. We put the revolver under the corner of our mattress and there it stayed. For ten days.

One night we went to the Fox Venice to see *Forbidden Planet*—you know, the movie about monsters from the id. When we returned, the door had been broken in. The stereo was gone, the television was gone, the paintings and cameras and typewriters were gone. The dressers had been turned over and ransacked, the bed had been torn up and the revolver taken; the birdcage had been torn off the wall and the parrakeet set free for a while until the cat got it and ate it, leaving the remains on the floor where a rug had been. All the jewelry was gone, such as it was. Including my Cartier watch. I had earned that watch, you know? I had saved for it just as surely as I had saved the money for a house or a car or a couple of new suits. That ended my romance with Cartier watches. There is an *enormous* black market for them in Los Angeles, but I don't want one now. I wear a Thirties Gruen Cruvex now, a sister to the watch Bogart wore in *Casablanca*. It's worth about the same as a tank watch but very few people *know what it is.*

Three thousand in after-tax dollars. It took the police two hours and forty-five minutes to show up.

Our revolver, which had begun as a museum piece, a curio, as far as we were concerned, had now entered the underworld. We were unprotected now, and we felt so. We reported the gun stolen, of course. Serial number and all that. Big deal. Five months later, it was used in an assault against a Los Angeles woman. I made up my mind that the way to handle a gun in a dangerous situation was to never let it out of my sight.

Our friends were robbed, burglarized. Carolyn, of her sewing machine, her typewriter, her clothes. Another couple, of all their photographic equipment, used not for a hobby but for their livelihood. Easy-going Boris bought a twelve-gauge riot gun and hid it in a trunk with his sixteen-millimeter movie equipment so no one would steal it. And a huge black shepherd dog to protect the trunk. Someone broke in anyway and slit the dog's throat.

We bought a new revolver, a .38 Special Smith & Wesson, and had the handgrips filed down so my wife could hold it easily. The two weeks while we waited for the permit to go through were the most terrifying of my life. . . .

A Purse Mugger

On the seventeenth of December in 1978, I saw a woman mugged for her purse—and I watched her run screaming after

Bob Dix, *Manchester Union Leader*. Reprinted with permission.

her assailant until she collapsed, crying in the street.

On the eighteenth or nineteenth of December, my wife was at a meeting, everybody else was busy doing something, and I walked alone to the Venice Sidewalk Cafe for some dinner. It occured to me that it was silly to put on a shoulder holster just to go out for a beer and a sandwich, but I did it anyway, although I had never been threatened physically, *ever*, except in foreign countries.

Walking home about six-thirty at night, just off the corner of West Washington Boulevard and Westminster Avenue, I was confronted by five young, well-dressed uptown brothers. Black. Okay. Let's get that right out front. *They could just as easily have been white.* We were directly under a streetlight and less than fifty feet from an intersection thick with traffic.

I was not dressed as a high roller. I am *not* a high roller. I don't look like a robber baron or a rich dentist. I look like exactly what I am, a middle-aged guy who's seen a little more than he needs to see. I thought, *what* are these guys *doing?*

Their leader pulled a kitchen knife out of his two-hundred-dollar leather jacket. His mistake was that he wasn't close enough to me to use it, only to threaten me. He smiled at me and said, "Just the wallet, man. Won't be no trouble."

That was a very long moment for me. I remember it just as it happened. I remember thinking at the time that it was one of those moments that are supposed to be charged with electricity. It wasn't. It was hollow, silent, and chilly.

I looked at this guy and at his companions and at his knife, and I thought: *Don't you see how you're misreading me? I am not a victim. I used to be a victim, but now I'm not. Can't you see the difference?*

I pulled the automatic, leveled it at them, and said very clearly, "You must be *dreaming*."

Killing for $35

The guy smiled at me and said "Sheeeit," and his buddies laughed, and he began to move toward me with the knife. I thought, this guy is willing to kill me for thirty-five dollars. I aimed the automatic at the outer edge of his left thigh and shot him.

He dropped like a high jumper hitting the bar and yelled "Goddamn!" three times, the first one from amazement, I guess, and the second two higher pitched and from pain.

He yelled at his buddies, "Ain't you gonna *do* nothing?" They did do nothing.

I backed off and I walked away, right across busy West Washington Boulevard, with the gun still in my hand. I remember thinking, shouldn't I call a doctor? And then I thought, would he have called a doctor for me? And I kept right on walking. . . .

I am not proud of this. I did not swallow it easily, either. More than a year passed before I talked about it with anybody, not even my wife. But I did it. And I could do it again if I had to.

Time's Swinging Door

What happened to us, of course, is that we got hit in the face with time's swinging door. The world changed sometime between 1975 and 1980, and we had a couple of tough years getting from one Pullman car to another. We were lucky. We lost more than eleven thousand dollars of what we owned, but we weren't killed. We adapted. Now the guns are a normal part of our lives. We accept them, just as we accept the seven motors of suburbia. They are a necessary convenience, like the washing machine or refrigerator or one of those devices that zaps mosquitoes with electricity.

Sometimes I think, this is a stupid, abhorrent, exasperating situation. And it is. But we've adpated to other stupid, abhor-rent, exasperating situations: 20 percent interest rates. Iran. And now we've adpated to this one.

Let me tell you how we've adapted. We dress low-key, we don't flaunt anything, we keep loaded guns in the house, and we don't keep them stashed in some drawer where we can't find them if we need them. We keep them right out in the open, and we always know *exactly* where they are. The difference is in that exterior framework of protection and in our attitudes toward it: it is something that was not necessary when we were younger, and it is something which most of us, . . .still carry on about. We don't even think it's too bad anymore; we're beyond that. We ac-cept it as a fact of life and go right on. And it will stay a fact of life until our fellow countrymen get it out of their heads that they can do as they please, that there is no such thing as social respon-sibility, that they have a *right* not to behave. Because, the way we see it, if they have the right to mug us, we have the right to shoot them.

Armed Criminals Terrify Citizens

The net effect of New York's stiff gun-control laws has put disarm-ed citizens at the mercy of criminals armed with illegal, black-marketed, unregistered, untraceable guns. Or turned otherwise law-abiding citizens into lawbreakers because they now own guns illegally out of desperation for their own protection and safety from runaway crime.

Phoebe Courtney, *The American Mercury*, Winter 1979.

I used to believe that these people had some justifications on their side. I used to feel that I ought to have some compassion for them, and I did. I used to believe that a job and some credit would put them on the right path. It isn't true. I also used to believe that much of the human wreckage—the millions upon millions of people with emotional damage—could be repaired. That isn't true either. They can't be, for the most part, because the effort necessary to straighten out a single one of them is enor-mous: four or five years perhaps of therapy, in an age when there is no time for anything but emergency medicine.

Stealing Because It Is Easy

Let's face it. Some of these people are poor. Some of them are driven crazy with desire for stuff they will never be able to af-ford. But not all of them are poor, not by a long shot. A lot of them make as much money, or a great deal more, than you or I do. They do it because it's *easy*. They do it because they believe no one will stop them. . . .

Now, about those fifty million handguns: taking them away will not automatically give us a society like England's or Holland's. We are just not like that. It would be nice if we were. That's why Americans run away to Europe. What might help is a good set of disk brakes on people's behavior here. But anything that might put such desperately needed stops on people's personal "freedoms" is perceived out there in the streets as a violation of civil liberties, of constitutional rights. That is, it is a "right" to mug, rape, burglarize, murder, and commit arson for the insurance money. So there you are: a nation of pirates.

I would like to see impossibly tight gun-registration laws, but I secretly scoff. Anyone who's honest can get through any registration process we can come up with. Anyone who's not honest won't bother. The way guns get into the criminal underworld is that they are *stolen*. That makes registration a useless exercise.

Arsenal of Democracy

As for the manufacture of all those devices and all those bullets, during World War II the United States became "The great arsenal of democracy." It is a damned good thing for the English that we were, too, or they would be holding Oktoberfests right now.

Do you really think the rest of the world sees us as insane because we bear arms? Try going to one of the South American countries. Try going into a country in which only the government has weapons. Try watching armed soldiers carrying their semiautomatic carbines around the airport gates and the customs offices, while the people have none. You want the wealth redistributed? Try it under *those* circumstances.

Don't talk to me about the saintly Japanese either. Everyone says they have a very low crime rate. No one really *knows*. It could be, because they are very big on making each person responsible for himself and also to his fellow countrymen: a sort of "One for all, all for one" attitude. They are sublimated like mad and they are rich because of it. It looks good on the surface, but just below that surface is a caldron: and if you look close you can see it. They have a history of barbarism that goes back for centuries and that we could never hope to match.

Needing a Good Gun

When the Soviets invaded Afghanistan, the first thing I thought was, now I'll never get to go there. Try putting yourself in Afghan shoes: no matter what you think, from your current vantage point, with a cellarful of good vintage wines and a wallful of Wittgenstein, if *you* lived there and the Soviets came trucking in with tanks and occupational forces, I am willing to bet you would hock your house, your automobile, your Baume & Mercier watch, or your ass on the street for a good gun and the bullets to put in it.

So much for international relations; on the home front, suffice it to say that as long as we live in a society in which a large constituency thinks it can do whatever it damn pleases—no sense of morality asked for or required—then those of us who have the middle-class work ethic, those of us who believe the Freudian epithets of work and love, will be seen as potential victims by the flocks of hustlers and lurkers who are out there. It *is* sometimes tough to get a job. It is also, right now, easier to rob people than it is to work for money. It's easier because it can be gotten away with. These people believe no one will stop them. They're right. No one will. Not the police, not the courts, not the penal system. No one but the growing number of us who have decided we will not be victimized again, ever.

"The 'right of the people to keep and bear arms,'. . . .belongs to each of us individually."

The Constitution Guarantees Personal Handguns

Dan Cohen

Dan Cohen is a free-lance copywriter in Minneapolis, Minnesota and is on the *Minneapolis Star Tribune's* Board of Contributors. A former public relations director for a Minneapolis advertising agency, he is active in area politics and was a former Republican mayoral candidate. In the following viewpoint, Mr. Cohen explains why he believes that gun control laws are an infringement upon the Second Amendment to the US Constitution.

As you read, consider the following questions:

1. How does the author compare the US and Britain homicide rates? Do you agree?
2. Mr. Cohen claims that the arguments of gun control proponents are emotional rather than rational. How would you classify his argument?
3. What three famous men does Mr. Cohen quote against gun control?

Dan Cohen, "Enforcing Gun Controls Would Trample Our Civil Liberties," *Minneapolis Star*, April 9, 1981. Reprinted with permission from the Minneapolis Star and Tribune.

People desperately want to understand the tragedies that affect their lives—even if there are no explanations. And it's a lot easier to identify the handgun, a recognizable symbol of death, as a cause of crime, than to admit we don't know the institutional and cultural factors that produce violence in our society.

How much better it makes us feel, how much more satisfying to say, "Who cares if handgun controls work or not, we've got to do something!" than to get embroiled in still another tedious dispute over the merits of gun controls and their probable effect.

And, too, there are those handgun prohibitionists who simply don't want to consider the merits of the argument. They are proud of their ignorance, because it demonstrates a revulsion against the hated gun that is so great that they're excused from having to react logically to the object of their displeasure.

Emotional Arguments

Thus, the Jerry Falwells of the world can pose as experts on pornography, tell us what we can and can't read, without having to paw through all that nasty stuff. Because the gun haters are so repelled by guns, because they cannot imagine why anyone would own one in the first place and, if so, why it shouldn't be taken from them, their attitude toward gun control is as realistic as someone's belief that accidental falls can be prevented by banning the law of gravity. Their emotions control their attitudes toward guns as much as any gun nut's emotions do.

This nation is not suffering from some kind of weapons sickness. About half the world's nations have homicide rates higher than ours. Gun control advocates, who rarely fail to point out that Britain, with strict handgun controls, has a lower homicide rate than we do, neglect the fact that the use of firearms in British crime was much less before 1920, when there were no controls of any sort, than it is today. Or that British homicide doubled in the period from 1960 to 1975, while the U.S. rates rose less than 30 percent. Or that we Americans also commit many more violent crimes without firearms. This raises the question: If firearms are the cause of firearms crimes, is it also the case that British criminals have access to fewer knives, clubs or hands and feet than Americans?

But why stop with Britain? Mexico has a homicide rate several times ours, though handgun legislation is restrictive. The rate of firearms ownership in Switzerland and Israel, with lower crime rates, well exceeds that of the United States, and moreover, these countries as well as several others, allow and even encourage widespread civilian ownership of fully automatic weapons.

Japan? That country has stricter gun controls and a lower homicide rate than the United States. Note, however, that

Japanese-Americans living in the weapons-mad United States have an even lower homicide rate than Japan's.

Gun Laws and Crime

And so it goes. The cities in the United States with the most violent crime tend to be those that are subject to the most restrictive gun laws. In the four years following the enactment of the Washington, D.C., restrictive gun law, the murder rate increased 18 percent, robbery 24 percent, and aggravated assault 34 percent.

Was the increase caused, as a Minneapolis editorial writer suggests, by the easy availabilty of guns in surrounding states? No. Guns were available in surrounding states prior to the enactment of the law, and during the three years just before the law was passed, the Washington crime rate actually fell.

The Sullivan Law, on the books in New York since 1910, has been almost totally ineffective in keeping guns out of the hands of New Yorkers. Today, they have an estimated 2 million illegal guns squirreled away. It's been argued that this could be prevented by national gun legislation of some kind—to prevent New Yorkers from buying guns in other states and bringing them back to New York. The fact is that such a practice is already illegal under federal law.

Amendment 2

A well-regulated militia, being necessary to the security of a free State, the right of the people to keep and bear arms, shall not be infringed.

Second Amendment to the Constitution of the United States.

The 1968 Gun Control Act contains a general prohibition against all transfers of firearms between residents of different states.

But, say the gun controllers, we haven't *really* tried. We haven't done all we could to eliminate handguns.

That's true.

Effective Control

And a measure of what can be done to get the 50 million or so handguns out of the hands of the public should be central to the argument over gun controls. For if both gun nuts and gun haters can agree that present-day gun control legislation in this country is ineffective, then we should consider just what it will take to make controls effective.

An official of the Police Federation, friendly to gun control, was questioned on this very point in an interview in the April 5 *New York Times*. He proposed that we adopt a stop-and-frisk system that would involve surprise spot checks of people, pedestrians and drivers, as they went about their daily business. Using the tools of modern technology, police would run them through portable metal detectors, like those found in airports, and some would be given a more thorough shakedown. He suggested that "high-crime" areas be targeted for this program.

It doesn't take much imagination to figure out where the "high-crime" areas are, or what kind of good, clean fun a Southern sheriff could have enforcing this kind of law. Or to imagine what the next step would be in achieving effective controls when criminals failed to cooperate by carrying handguns in their hip pockets or glove compartments: National ID cards? House-to-house searches? Police raids on clubs, offices, public gatherings? A national network of informants? Wiretaps?

Guns Deter Violence

Nor should we fail to mention that one reason the Klan and its cohorts failed to intimidate Southern blacks during the civil rights unrest of the 1960s as they had in the 1880s was not the vigilance of Southern police departments in protecting black citizens. It was because behind many a door in the black section of town was many a handgun. And the Klan knew it.

US Constitution Supports Guns

And what about the Second Amendment, the one that's supposed to protect the ". . .right of the people to keep and bear arms." Legal scholars are divided over whether this is a collective or individual right, but I submit, that like the ". . .right of the people" to be free from unreasonable searches and seizures, it belongs to each of us individually.

Dan Cohen, *Minneapolis Star,* April 9, 1981.

There is simply no way to get handguns away from a vast part of the American population without doing violence to civil liberties, the Fourth Amendment protection against unreasonable searches and seizures and condoning the excesses of cruel and indifferent authorities.

And what about the Second Amendment, the one that's supposed to protect the ". . .right of the people to keep and bear arms." Legal scholars are divided over whether this is a collective or individual right, but I submit, that like the ". . .right of the people" to be free from unreasonable searches and seizures, it belongs to each of us individually.

169

In fact, a few other rednecks have seemed to share my distrust of the benign protective power of government to save us from ourselves. Let me quote a few:

Mahatma Gandhi: "Among the many misdeeds of British rule in India, history will look upon the Act depriving a whole nation of arms as the blackest."

Hubert H. Humphrey: "The right of citizens to bear arms is just one more guarantee against arbitrary government, one more safeguard against the tyranny that now appears remote in America, but that historically has proved to be always possible."

Thomas Jefferson: ". . .And what country can preserve its liberties if its rulers are not warned from time to time that this people preserve the spirit of resistance. Let them take arms."

"The Second Amendment does not give anyone the right to personal possession of weapons."

The Constitution Does Not Guarantee Personal Handguns

Denis Wadley

Denis Wadley is an English instructor at De LaSalle High School in Minneapolis, Minnesota and an officer of Americans for Democratic Action. As a member of the *Minneapolis Star Tribune's* board of contributors, he submitted an article he authored from which the following viewpoint is excerpted. In it, Mr. Wadley illustrates why he believes that the Second Amendment to the Constitution does not give citizens the right to personal possession of handguns.

As you read, consider the following questions:

1. Why does the author think gun control laws are essential?
2. In what ways does he say opponents of gun control misinterpret the Constitution?
3. How does the author think gun control laws could be useful in crime detection?

Denis Wadley, "Gun-Related Crime Soars, But NRA Still Calls the Shots," *Minneapolis Star*, February 3, 1982. Reprinted with permission from the Minneapolis Star and Tribune.

171

At least once a month for years now, some paper or news program has featured a shooting, almost always domestic, that simply wouldn't have happened had firearms not been so easily obtainable. In any other area, from medicine to building codes, so easily identifiable a cause would long since have been addressed by law.

It hasn't been dealt with because of well-financed lobbying by the National Rifle Association and its allied groups, several misconceptions about weapons and the right to own them, and one very strong argument that has yet to be answered by gun opponents.

The NRA has been panicking on cue for years about how a disarmed nation is easy prey for communists and criminals, and has retailed slogans at the rate of two or three new ones per annum about self-protection and constitutional rights.

Legislators have listened to the NRA not because its arguments make sense, but because it has money and has organized local gun fanciers to show up at public hearings, giving elected representatives the impression that they speak for vast numbers of people.

Well, they don't. All the surveys indicate that these people represent a steadily decreasing minority that is, accordingly, getting louder and more hysterical. The NRA is a paper tiger, and the sooner Congress and the state legislatures realize that, the sooner some attempt will be made to solve the firearms problem.

To drive an auto or a motorcycle, one must show sufficient skill and knowledge to pass a test. To own a gun—and in industrialized nations guns have killed far more people than cars and cycles have, even disallowing wars—one need only buy it in most places, and in a few others wait a short time.

The Unites States is the only major nation to have no significant gun control laws. And, as a direct result, we have the highest level of domestic violence in the industrialized world.

Constitutional Arguments

One of the tired arguments against gun control involves the Constitution. A person fanatically convinced of something can usually find it validated in either the Bible or the Constitution, whether the proof is there or not.

The Second Amendment does not give anyone the right to personal possession of weapons. The text is short: "A well-regulated militia, being necessary to the security of a free state, the right of the people to keep and bear arms shall not be infringed."

The article relates entirely to the militia—a fact made even clearer by a clause dropped by Congress from James Madison's original wording: ". . .but no person religiously scrupulous of bearing arms should be compelled to render military service in

172

person.''

In "The Bill of Rights: Its Origin and Meaning," historian Irving Brant notes: "The Second Amendment [is] popularly misread. . .[Its intent] was made clearest of all in the congressional debate on the amendment. Why was a militia necessary to the 'security of a free state'? Elbridge Gerry asked and answered that question: 'What, sir, is the use of a militia? It is to prevent the establishment of a standing army, the bane of liberty.'

"Thus, the purpose of the Second Amendment was to forbid Congress to prohibit the maintenance of a state militia. By its nature that amendment cannot be transformed into a personal right to bear arms, enforceable by federal compulsion upon the states."

One wonders how many of the gun defenders favor such weapons "to prevent the establishment of a standing army." Quite the reverse, it would seem.

Supreme Court's Interpretation

In 1967 the President's Commission on Law Enforcement and Administration of Justice concluded emphatically that "The U.S. Supreme Court and lower Federal courts have consistently interpreted this Amendment only as a prohibition against Federal interference with State militia and not as a guarantee of an individual's right to keep or carry firearms."

Raymond Rogers, *Vital Speeches of the Day*, October 1, 1983.

The Supreme Court has ruled on several occasions that this is the proper view of the Second Amendment. No federal court has ever ruled any other way. The latest such ruling came only recently when the Supreme Court unanimously upheld the constitutionality of the city ordinance passed in Morton Grove, Ill., prohibiting the possession or use of handguns by private citizens within the town limits.

The landmark case is United States vs. Miller (1939). The ruling sustained the National Firearms Act of 1934, which levied a virtually prohibitive tax on concealable weapons and required their registration. It makes perfectly clear that the Second Amendment does not apply to concealed weapons, but asserts only the right to bear them openly as part of a militia.

We are told on bumper stickers that "when guns are outlawed, only outlaws will have guns," a tautological phrase influential only for those who don't think it through.

In England, the fact that the police don't carry guns has not resulted in a proliferation of firearms; on the contrary, possession of guns has been restrained. In those nations where only the police are armed, there still is not the high incidence of gun ownership that exists in the United States, which has almost no legal restraints.

Laws Prevent Crime

Such laws can help prevent crime. Without them, law enforcement officials must wait until someone commits a crime—or is clearly just about to—before taking action. With strong controls, the mere possession of a gun, unless registered or licensed, would be a crime, and police officers would gain a handle on possibly dangerous situations.

Gun control laws are also useful in crime detection. In the celebrated trial of Angela Davis a few years back, California officials testified in court that the only reason Davis could be arrested and brought to trial at all was that the murder weapon in the case had been registered and was known to be hers.

Moreover, in California a person is responsible for what happens with his firearm even if he isn't in possession of it.

Most of the killings in the United States, in all recent years surveyed, were committed with handguns. Of those, a preponderance were committed by people without criminal records—good citizens—either by accident or in a fit of passion with a gun nearby.

Gun advocates cannot get around the blunt fact that if the guns weren't there, they couldn't be used.

A gun is the only instrument of murder that need not be close to the victim to be effective. Canards about outlawing knives, poison or clubs next—the old "slippery slope" argument—make no sense, because the weapons aren't comparable.

Gun control legislation would be obeyed by good citizens, yes. And by doing so they would eliminate the vast majority of deaths by firearms in this country.

Recognizing Statements That Are Provable

From various sources of information we are constantly confronted with statements and generalizations about social and moral problems. In order to think clearly about these problems, it is useful if one can make a basic distinction between statements for which evidence can be found and other statements which cannot be verified or proved because evidence is not available, or the issue is so controversial that it cannot be definitely proved.

Readers should constantly be aware that magazines, newspapers and other sources often contain statements of a controversial nature. The following activity is designed to allow experimentation with statements that are provable and those that are not.

Most of the following statements are taken from the viewpoints in this chapter. Consider each statement carefully. *Mark P for any statement you believe is provable. Mark U for any statement you feel is unprovable because of the lack of evidence. Mark C for statements you think are too controversial to be proved to everyone's satisfaction.*

If you are doing this activity as a member of a class or group, compare your answers with those of other class or group members. Be able to defend your answers. You may discover that others will come to different conclusions than you. Listening to the reasons others present for their answers may give you valuable insights in recognizing statements that are provable.

If you are reading this book alone, ask others if they agree with your answers. You too will find this interaction very valuable.

P = provable
U = unprovable
C = too controversial

1. When criminals know that someone can handle a gun, they are far less willing to make him or her their victim.

2. A gun kept for protection is six times more likely to kill someone you know rather than an attacker.

3. Tough laws against the gun will not reduce crime and violence in the United States.

4. People *with* guns do the most robbing and killing in the United States.

5. A handgun is a very poor defensive weapon.

6. The average perpetrator of a crime of passion is a violent sociopath—just the type of person least likely to obey gun laws.

7. Of the fifteen states with the highest homicide rates, ten have restrictive or very restrictive gun laws.

8. Gun prohibitionists tend to focus on foreign examples which support their thesis, and ignore the rest.

9. Guns don't kill people, people kill people.

10. Gun laws do not deter criminals.

11. It is, right now, easier to rob people than it is to work for money.

12. About half the world's nations have homicide rates higher than ours.

13. There is simply no way to get handguns away from a vast part of the American population without doing violence to civil liberties.

14. The Second Amendment does not give anyone the right to personal possession of weapons.

15. To own a gun, one need only buy it in most cities, and in a few others wait a short time.

Bibliography

The following list of periodical articles deals with the subject matter of this chapter.

Leonard Berkowitz   "How Guns Control Us," *Psychology Today*, June 1981.

Ted Gest   "Battle Over Gun Control Heats Up Across U.S.," *U.S. News & World Report*, May 31, 1982.

David Hardy   "Why Gun Control Can't Work: What We've Learned in New York and Hawaii, *Inquiry*, February 28, 1982.

Mark Hendrickson   "In Defense of Handguns," *The New Guard*, Summer 1982.

Don B. Kates, Jr.   "Gun Control: Can It Work?" *National Review*, May 15, 1981.

Robert Kubey   "Instead of Handguns," *Newsweek*, September 20, 1982.

Lance Morrow   "It's Time to Ban Handguns," *Time*, April 13, 1981.

The Nation   "Equal Protection," May 16, 1983.

Charles J. Orasin   "Holstering America's Handguns," *New York Times*, September 8, 1983.

Donald D. Schroeder   "What's Your Source of Protection?" *The Plain Truth*, June 1983.

Aric Press and Others   "The Plague of Violent Crime," *Newsweek*, March 23, 1981.

Thomas J. Ruse   "Demythologizing Crime," *America*, March 24, 1984.

Time   "Street Sentence: Vigilante Justice in Buffalo," August 15, 1983.

Frank Trippett   "A Red Light for Scofflaws," *Time*, January 24, 1983.

James Q. Wilson   "Thinking About Crime," *The Atlantic Monthly*, September 1983.

Organizations to Contact

American Civil Liberties Union
22 East 40th St.
New York, NY 10016
(212) 944-9800

One of America's oldest civil liberties organizations. Founded in 1920, the ACLU champions the rights set forth in the Declaration of Independence and the Constitution. The Foundation of the ACLU provides legal defense, research, and education. It publishes the quarterly newspaper *Civil Liberties* and various pamphlets, books, and position papers.

American Correctional Association
4321 Hartwick Rd.
College Park, MD 20740
(301) 699-7600

A membership organization of practitioners and academicians in the corrections field. The ACA provides timely materials on theoretical and practical aspects of criminal justice and corrections. Publishes *Corrections Today.*

American Judicature Society
200 W. Monroe St.
Suite 1606
Chicago, IL 60606
(312) 558-6900

A group of lawyers, judges, law teachers, government officials and citizens interested in the effective administration of justice. The society conducts research, offers a consultation service, works to combat court congestion and delay, and sponsors essay contests for law and graduate students. Publishes *Judicature.*

American Justice Institute
725 University Ave.
Sacramento, CA 95825
(916) 924-3700

Works to reduce crime, delinquency and related social problems. Provides public and private justice agencies with statistics, demonstrations and assistance in training and evaluation.

American Police Reserves Association
615 Headquarters Bldg.
Washington, DC 20036

An association concerned with the constitutional rights and protection of life and property during any national emergency or natural disaster, where governments may need police reserves. This association was founded to encourage the formation of units of police reserves.

Christic Institute
1324 Capitol St.
Washington, DC 20002
(202) 797-8106

Engages in litigation for persons who cannot afford legal representation in matters concerning social justice or empowerment in the democratic process, in the defense of human and civil rights, and in support of peace and ecology issues.

Contact Inc.
PO Box 81826
Lincoln, NE 68501

An international, non-profit criminal justice information clearinghouse founded in 1964. Publishes *Corrections Compendium*.

Defense Research Institute
733 North Van Buren St.
Milwaukee, WI 53202
(414) 272-5995

Founded in 1960, the institute carries out a program of education and information against abuses in the compensation of personal injury claimants. Seeks to increase the knowledge and improve the skills of defense lawyers and improve the adversary system.

The Fellowship of Reconciliation
Box 271
Nyack, NY 10960
(914) 358-4601

The Fellowship, founded in England in 1914, works to abolish war and advocates methods of dealing with offenders against society that will seek to redeem and rehabilitate rather than to impose punishment. FOR also supports the elimination of capital punishment.

The Fortune Society
229 Park Ave. S.
New York, NY 10003
(212) 677-4600

Composed of ex-convicts and others interested in penal reform. The Society educates and trains ex-convicts and helps them find jobs and readjust to society.

Friends Outside
116 E. San Luis St.
Salinas, CA 93901
(408) 758-2733

A non-profit organization that works to place staff prison representatives inside prisons to provide a liason between the inmates and their families.

HALT: Americans for Legal Reform
201 Massachusetts Ave., NE
Suite 319
Washington, DC 20002
(202) 546-4258

A service organization with a national membership of 120,000. The organization seeks to relieve the average citizen of the oppressive cost of a lawyer and the lengthy procedural entanglements of litigation. HALT believes that many transactions can be handled with minimal or no lawyer intervention.

National Association of Juvenile Correctional Agencies
36 Locksley Ln.
Springfield, IL 62704
(217) 787-0690

Founded in 1959, the association disseminates ideas on the philosophy, goals and functions of the juvenile correctional field with an emphasis on institutional rehabilitative programs.

National Association on Volunteers in Criminal Justice
PO Box 6365
University, AL 35486
(205) 348-6738

Committed to the improvement of the juvenile and criminal justice systems through the development and support of citizen participation. The association provides technical assistance, education, and training on volunteerism.

National Council on Crime and Delinquency
Continental Plaza
411 Hackensack Ave.
Hackensack, NJ 07601
(201) 488-0400

Organization of Social workers, corrections, specialists and others interested in community based programs, juvenile and family courts, and the prevention, control and treatment of crime and delinquency. Publishes a multitude of publications including *Crime and Delinquency.*

National Criminal Justice Association
444 North Capitol St., NW
Suite 305
Washington, DC 20001
(202) 347-4900

Provides a forum for development and expression of unified state views on criminal and juvenile justice issues. Its objectives are to focus attention on controlling crime and improving individual states' administration of their criminal and juvenile justice systems.

National Institute of Victimology
2333 N. Vernon St.
Arlington, VA 22207
(703) 528-8872

Founded in 1976, the institute works to improve victim/witness services and to make the public and criminal justice personnel aware of the needs of crime victims. Publishes *Victimology: an International Journal.*

National Moratorium on Prison Construction
324 C St., SE
Washington, DC 20003
(202) 547-3633

Engages in public education, lobbying and direct action to stop construction of new prisons and jails. Gathers, analyzes, and disseminates information about prison and jail construction plans on the federal, state, and local levels. Publishes *JERICHO.*

National Organization for Victim Assistance
1757 Park Rd., NW
Washington, DC 20010
(202) 232-8560

Serves as a national forum for victim advocacy by providing direct services to victims of crime where no services exist, providing education and technical assistance to service providers on victim issues and serving as a membership organization for the general public who support the victims movement.

National Institute For Citizen Education in the Law
605 G St., NW No. 401
Washington, DC 20001
(202) 624-8217

The institute educates the public about practical ("street") law in the areas of criminal, consumer, housing, family and individual rights. Assists law schools in conducting law-related courses in elementary and secondary settings. Publishes *Street Law News.*

Offender Aid and Restoration
Historic Albermarle County Jail
409 East High St.
Charlottesville, VA 22901
(804) 295-6196

A community-based movement of volunteers that aid prisoners and ex-prisoners in making the transition from prison to outside. The organization is also involved in jail reform.

People for the American Way
1015 18th St., NW
Suite 300
Washington, DC 20036
(202) 822-9450

A nonprofit, nonpartisan education organization that works to protect all Americans' individual rights and freedoms from extremist attacks. Involved in three major program areas: mass media, communications, citizen action and public education.

The Police Executive Research Forum
1909 K St., NW
Suite 400
Washington, DC 20006
(202) 466-7820

A membership organization for police chief executives. Provides support services to members, including consulting and research projects. Maintains a central clearinghouse for police research information.

VERA Institute of Justice
30 E 39th St.
New York, NY 10016
(212) 986-6910

Conducts action-research projects in criminal justice reform. Projects include the Manhattan Bail Project which made recommendations to the court and the Victim/Witness Assistance Project which provide services to victims and civilian police prosecution witnesses.

Washington Crime News Services
From the State Capitols
Published by Wakeman/Walworth Inc.
PO Box 1939
New Haven, CT 06509
(203) 562-8518

A series of newsletters that track the activities of state legislatures, regional committees, city planners, courts and other agencies.

Bibliography of Books

Peter Arnold

Crime and Youth: A Practical Guide to Crime Prevention. New York: Julian Mossner, 1976.

Howard Ball

Courts and Politics: The Federal Judicial System. Englewood Cliffs, NJ: Prentice-Hall, 1980.

Gregg Barak

In Defense of Whom? A Critique of Criminal Justice Reform. Cincinnati: Anderson Publishing, 1980.

Abraham S. Blumberg

Current Perspectives on Criminal Behavior. New York: Alfred A. Knopf, 1974.

Stanley L. Brodsky

Psychologists in the Criminal Justice System. Champaign, IL: University of Illinois Press, 1973.

Edmund Cahn

Right and Wrong in the Light of American Law. Bloomington: Indiana University Press, 1981.

Frank Carrington and William Lambie

Defenseless Society, Aurora, IL: Green Hill, 1976.

Gary Cavender

Parole: A Critical Analysis. Port Washington, NY: Kennikat Press, 1982.

Francis T. Cullen

Reaffirming Rehabilitation. Cincinnati: Anderson Publishing, 1982.

Thomas E. Davitt

Basic Values in Law—A Study of the Ethics, Milwaukee: Marquette University Press, 1968.

Department of Justice, State of California

Crime and Delinquency in California. Pamphlet available from Department of Justice, 3301 C St., P.O. 13427, Sacramento, CA 95813. 1981.

Richard DiPrima

First Amendment. Madison, WI: Educational Industries Inc., 1982.

James O. Finkenauer

Scared Straight and the Panacea Phenomenon. Englewood Cliffs, NJ: Prentice-Hall, 1982.

James F. Gilginan

Doing Justice: How the System Works, As Seen by the Participants. Englewood Cliffs, NJ: Prentice-Hall, 1982.

G. Thomas Goodnight and David Hingston — *The Question of Justice: A Basic Overview of the Problems Involved in the US Judicial System*. Lincolnwood, IL: National Textbook Co., 1983.

Mark J. Green and Bruce Wasserstein — *With Justice for Some: An Indictment of the Law by Young Advocates*. Boston: Beacon Press, 1972.

HALT Inc. — *Probate; Shopping for a Lawyer; Victims' Rights*. Pamphlets available from HALT Inc., An Organization of Americans for Legal Reform, 201 Massachusetts Ave. NE, Washington, DC 20002.

Mary Ann Harrell and Burnett Anderson — *Equal Justice Under Law: The Supreme Court in American Life*. Washington, DC: The Supreme Court Historical Society in cooperation with the National Geographic Society, 1982.

Daryl A. Hellman — *The Economics of Crime*, New York: St. Martin, 1980.

Thomas J. Hynes, Jr. and William F. Campbell — *One Justice for All! A Critical Analysis of the Problems Involved in the US Judicial System*. Lincolnwood, IL: National Textbook Co., 1983.

Dave Jackson — *Dial 911: Peaceful Christians and Urban Violence*. Chicago: Herald Press, 1982.

Herbert Jacob — *Urban Justice: Law and Order in American Cities*. Englewood Cliffs, NJ: Prentice-Hall, 1973.

Gary Kinder — *Victim: the Other Side of Murder*. New York: Delacorte Press, 1982.

Sidney Langer — *Scared Straight; Fear in the Deterrence of Delinquency*. Lanham, MD: University Press of America, 1982.

Robert Lehrman — *Doing Time; A Look at Crime and Prisons*. New York: Hastings House Publishing, 1980.

Cesare Lombroso — *The Origin of the Causes of Crime*. Albuquerque: American Classical College Press, 1982.

Doug McGee — *Slow Coming Dark: Interviews from Death Row*. New York: Pilgrim Press, 1980.

Carl Martin — *To Hell with the Constitution: An Expose*. Toledo, OH: Commonsense, 1971.

Andre Mayer and Michael Wheller
The Crocodile Man: A Case of Brain Chemistry and Criminal Violence. Easton, PA: Houghton Mifflin, 1982.

Karl Menninger
The Crime of Punishment. New York: The Viking Press, 1968.

Sandra J. Merwin
Not A Victim: Prevent Violent Crime from Happening to You! Minneapolis, MN: EM Press, 1982.

J.L. Miller
Sentencing Reform: A Review and Annotated Bibliography. Williamsburg, VA: National Center for the State Courts, 1981.

Harry More
Critical Issues in Law Enforcement. Cincinnati: Anderson Publishing, 1981.

Gerhard Mueller
Comparative Criminal Law in the United States. Littleton, CO: Rothmar, 1970.

Geoff Munghan and Zenon Bankowski
Essays in Law and Society. Boston: Routledge and Kegan, 1980.

National Coalition for Jail Reform
Juveniles and Jail; LOOK at Your Jail; Jail, the New Mental Institution; Pretrial Detention: Waiting for Justice; The Public Inebriate, Jail Is Not the Answer. Pamphlets available from National Coalition for Jail Reform, 1828 L Street, NW, Washington, DC 20036.

National Criminal Justice Association
Illegal Drug Trafficking in the United States. Pamphlet available from NCJA, 444 North Capitol St. NW, Suite 305, Washington, DC 20001.

Charm Perelman
Justice, Law and Argument: Essays on Moral and Legal Reasoning. Boston: Keuwer, 1980.

William H. Parsonage
Perspectives on Victimology. Beverly Hills, CA: Sage Publishing, 1979.

Chapman Pincher
Their Trade Is Treachery. New York: Bantam Books Inc., 1982.

Fritz Redl and David Wineman
Children Who Hate: The Disorganization and Breakdown of Behavior Controls. New York: Free Press, 1965.

Helen Reynolds
Cops and Dollars: The Economics of Criminal Law and Justice. Springfield, IL: Charles C. Thomas Publishing Co., 1981.

Pamela Richards
Crime as Play: Delinquency in a Middle Class Suburb. Cambridge: Ballinger Press, 1979.

Albert R. Roberts
Correctional Treatment of the Offender: A Book of Readings. Springfield, IL: Charles C. Thomas, 1974.

Parker Rossman

After Punishment, What? Discipline and Reconciliation. Cleveland, OH: Collins Publishing, 1980.

Ann Z. Shanks

Busted Lives: Dialogues with Kids in Jail. New York: Delacorte Press, 1982.

David Schichor and Delos H. Kelly

Critical Issues in Juvenile Delinquency. Lexington, MA: Lexington Books, 1980.

Steven Schlossman

Love and the American Delinquent: The Theory and Practice of "Progressive" Juvenile Justice. Chicago: University of Chicago Press, 1981.

Edwin Schur and Hugo A. Bedau

Victimless Crimes: Two Sides of A Controversy. Englewood Cliffs, NJ: Prentice-Hall, 1974.

Martin D. Schwartz

Corrections: An Issues Approach. Cincinnati: Anderson Publishing Co., 1980.

Edward J. Shaughnessy

Bail and Preventive Detention in New York. Lanham, MD: University Press of America, 1982.

Charles E. Silberman

Criminal Violence, Criminal Justice. New York: Random House, 1978.

Henry J. Steadman

Beating A Rap? Defendants Found Incompetent to Stand Trial. Chicago: University of Chicago Press, 1979.

D. H. Stott

Delinquency: The Problem and Its Prevention. Jamaica, NY: S.P. Medical and Science Books, 1982.

Ann Strick

Injustice for All: How Our Adversary System of Law Victimizes Us and Subverts True Justice. New York: Penguin, 1978.

United States General Accounting Office

Improved Federal Efforts Needed to Change Juvenile Detention Practices. Pamphlet available from General Accounting Office, Information Handling and Support Facility, Document Handling and Information Service Component, Box 6015, Gaithersburg, MD 20877.

Andrew H. Vachss

The Life Style Violent Juvenile: The Secure Treatment Approach. Lexington, MA: Lexington Books, 1979.

Stephen VanDine

Restraining the Wicked: The Incapacitation of The Dangerous Criminal. Lexington, MA: Lexington Books, 1979.

Index